A CHRISTMAS CRACKER OF EVENTS, HAPPENINGS ... AND SPECIAL SERVICES SO THAT CHRISTMAS IS NEVER MIS-SPENT

ROBERT PARKER

Published by Robert Parker 2022

ISBN: 978-1-915351-08-1

Printed by
DolmanScott
www.dolmanscott.co.uk

FOREWORD TO A CHRISTMAS CRACKER

Isn't it remarkable? Here's an old priest who's still imaginative, still playful, still full of a sacred mischief. He's "Tigger" in A. A. Milne. And he still, maybe more than ever, believes that the birth of the Christ is about all of us, that the Christ comes alive in us, by 'peep' and 'popper' all of the time. To put it another way, Robert Parker will never let the liturgies of the Church become burial rites. They're about life; okay, life Good Friday by Good Friday, though Easter by Easter. Maybe, when we were kids, we didn't get it. Now we do. All the better to make every Sunday a splurge of loving. That's what A CHRISTMAS CRACKER is about.

A CHRISTMAS CRACKER, by title, announces "EVENTS, HAPPENINGS & SPECIAL SERVICES." You could conclude that it's a 'how-to' book and put it down. Don't. Ransack this book. To be very honest with you, this is a treatise about epistemology. Keep reading. This is a book about how we learn things, how we understand things, how we make those things useful for our living. It is not achieved passively. It's achieved actively. In church, say, you dress up like Mary or Joseph or a shepherd or a Wise Man, you march around, you say things and sing, you wrap a box in Christmas paper and unwrap it to the Christ Child within. The memory, from childhood to old age, is in your eyes, in your ears, in your nose, in your hands and feet. It's part of you, intellectually, emotionally, spiritually. It's somehow you, accessible whenever – or especially – when darkness falls and you're down.

In A CHRISTMAS CRACKER, Robert Parker will tell you how to. He knows how to. I think you'd be smart to give some things a try. There's a lot to be gained.

I incite you to get going with this book, all the way back to "Epoch 1 – Hell on Earth" and "Epoch 2 – The Birth of Christ." This is powerful stuff. Robert gets passionate here; he's poetic. There's terror ("PAIN") and there's a hope that turns to salvation. If the problem of Christianity is "to convert Christians to it," as Soren Kierkegaard said, here's something that will do it. I plan to use "Epoch 1" and "Epoch 2" with an adult group I lead.

I know the author, Robert Parker, well. And I'd like to know the author of his life and mine better than I do. A CHRISTMAS CRACKER will urge me on. Mid-way through this book, I realized that it's a treasure. It's far more than one man's learning and one man's inventions. It's about one man's soul.

The Rt. Rev. John S. Thornton (Retired bishop of Idaho)

Christmas is exciting, and when it comes to worship in Church or school, it can also be very challenging. Over many years of leading worship I have discovered that it is possible to create a sense of wonder, awe and excitement within these services. When it happens it is extremely thrilling for all concerned, and when a great number of youngsters of all ages are involved, it can be quite electrifying. I felt that I would like to share some of my experiences with you. I hope that as you read what follows you will feel stimulated to create your own events and special services but will perhaps wish to borrow extensively from all that follows. I also hope that you will enjoy yourselves immensely.

As we explore our relationship with God, people are led along paths that are as varied as the individual characteristics and ideas of each person. Each and every path can lead to moments of personal discovery, and with these discoveries comes satisfaction, great humour and joy.

I think that he has just had a moment of personal discovery

The ideas that follow are an attempt to demonstrate how different congregations have explored the God/Man relationship. For some readers, these events and the methods used to drive them may give no insight at all into the meaning of Christmas, but for others I hope that they will be hugely stimulated and want to become creative in their own way – and that is the main purpose of this book.

The book is divided into 3 parts:

Section 1 is an event which can fill the "Sermon Slot" in a family service or a school assembly, whether it is a Eucharist or another form of worship. It can be at any time of day: morning, afternoon or evening. Some of this section needs almost no preparation and could be a great boon to the overburdened parson, headmaster or preacher who, after years of dedicated work, feels that he or she is either "drying up": or lacks the time to search for, and / or create, new ideas.

I wish the vicar would stop all these stupid surprises ... and just get on with the service!

Section 2. This section is made up of a number of complete services, each of which can stand in its own right. The first two services in this section are presented with guidelines as to how to develop them. The other four are actual services and are presented just as they have occurred, and are therefore reproduced in full. In this way, the reader can see why and how they happened.

I would expect that most of those who choose to use one or more of them will wish to make massive changes and adaptations to suit their own particular situation. I invite you to use any one of the services in full if you wish to do so, or merely to take it as the germ of an idea, to be developed and used in whatever appropriate way resonates with you and in your own setting.

Section 3. This section contains some ideas for embellishing both sections 1 & 2 or simply using them on their own. Many of these ideas can also be interwoven with other themes created by the reader. These ideas, just like the sermon slots and the services, have brought a huge amount of joy and fun to the great many people with whom I have shared them. But please, please, don't be bound by what I have done. Use the book in your own way to reach out to others, and so engage with them as they try to find and explore their own relationship with God.

CONTENTS

SECTION 1 ... PAGE 1

SECTION 2: INTRODUCTION ... PAGE 49

SECTION 3: MISCELLANEOUS IDEAS ... PAGE 109

SECTION 1

PREPARE YE THE WAY OF THE LORD

Theme

Have you ever asked yourself the question 'How does one put across to children the idea that, at the beginning of time, there was darkness?' (the Bible tells us 'There was darkness over the water'); that there was no life, nothing at all … just emptiness; The universe, as it then existed at the very beginning of time, was black, empty and desolate. It needed God to breathe into this emptiness the power of life, through His Spirit. His power came into the nothingness, and as that happened so began creation … Indeed, Christians believe this 'breathing of God's spirit' had to happen for there ever to be any kind of creation or life at all. So how does one put across that concept, and how does one share that idea with a child? Well, perhaps we begin by exploring the fact that all of us … even children, experience moments of great darkness or deep despair … a time when it feels as if God is absent … And that is like nothingness, or 'pre-creation' …

1 **Turn off every light so that the Church is in complete darkness, there is inky blackness everywhere**
For the Native tribes of America, fear and evil and death are represented by total darkness. The North American Natives won't go out at night because they believe that evil roams abroad. (Read the poem *Hiawatha*)

2 **Light a taper, and then from it, one single candle in the Chancel**
Creation is the coming of life and light. Creation is the bringing of order from chaos. It is God breathing his Spirit of Life into the darkness. Then, this Spirit of Life is passed on into our own individual persona; into our bodies and into our minds and spirit, and this 'persona' is created in us whether we are Christians or have another faith, or none at all. Because of Christmas, we Christians believe that Jesus has been sent into the world as the Saviour … the Bible uses the word 'Christ' as the one who comes as the light of the world, to bring a new meaning to Creation. The Creative process was begun by God, at the very first moment in time. And so creation was begun, and our world, our solar system, our galaxy (of which there are many) was a part of this creation. Many millions of years after the creative process began, Jesus comes to our world at Christmas, the darkest time of the year, to bring light to the world. As Christians we believe that he came to save the world from the 'darkness'.

The darkness represents evil, sin and selfishness; Jesus comes to bring a new, vivid, and startling light, so that all the people of the world can see God and come to God. Yet, sadly, many people are afraid to face this light (God) because they know that once they are bathed in the light of God, that their dark lives of sin and selfishness might be exposed. If that happens, it means that their dark lives will be exposed to all the people around them, and to God himself. For that reason, they prefer to operate in darkness, so that their sin, their failure, is hidden or covered up.

3   **Ask everyone to stand and then turn away from the light and turn back again to face it, and do this three times**
However, at various times in our lives most of us realise that there are dark situations that we are facing when we need light to live, and so we turn back to God. Turning round to face God is the literal interpretation of the word "repentance". This process brings new life to all. This new life is infectious, catching, spreading, and creative. It is life, and just like a brilliant light (a meteor entering the Earth's atmosphere) can be spread to the four corners of the earth.

4   **The light then spreads from the Chancel to the whole Church as first a number of people standing in the aisle light a taper, and then, moving through the Church, everyone present lights their own candle (or night light) from the tapers which have taken their light from the one lighted candle in the chancel**

Has anyone in the congregation got a match?

Drama / Presentation

1   The Church in darkness – totally black
2   One light in the Chancel
3   People turn to face the light, turn away from the light, and then repeat this three times
4   The light is then spread from the Chancel, through the whole Church
    (It is passed from person to person, each holding a candle / taper / night light)

Visual Aids / Props Needed

Candles, tapers, matches

Optional: one candle or light for everyone

Alternatively, use the Church main lights, instead of candles if necessary, turning them on in different parts of the Church at the appropriate moment

NO 2
ADVENT CANDLES

Theme

Paula was born in Frankfurt, Germany. She came to England just before the First World War began to train to be a nurse. She stayed in an English home, living with an English family. On the first Advent Sunday that she was here, she went to her room to fetch her 'Advent Candles' which she had brought with her from Germany and took them down to show her English hosts.

The English couple had never seen anything like this before. Paula explained to the fascinated pair that each of the candles represented one of the Sundays in Advent and symbolised the nearness of the coming of Christ. She explained that the celebration of the birth of Jesus was only four weeks away, and now was the time to start preparing for His coming.

The first candle, to be lit on the first Sunday of Advent, symbolised that God was coming to the earth as a man. **(Light first candle)**

God gives light to the world.

The second candle reminds us of where we look to find out what God has done through history and is still doing today **(light second candle)**. We refer to the Bible, and we call this day Bible Sunday. The Bible is revered as the word of God. We use the Bible both in Church and at home, because it explains the way that God has shown to mankind what kind of God He is, and how men and women have responded to the revelation of Himself, and all that He has done, and still does today.

On the third Sunday the theme revolves around the cousin of Jesus who was named John. Later he was called John the Baptist, and this is how the Bible refers to him. John the Baptist calls every one of us to prepare for the coming of Jesus **(light third candle)**. So, if John called us to prepare, How do we do it?

We use puddings, presents, Christmas tree, cakes, and carols. Yes, of course … and all that is good. But our preparation must also include looking at what we ourselves have become, all our mistakes and failings … and if we do that properly then we should feel the emotion called 'repentance' … The meaning of that word is literally … 'Turn round and face God.' We must therefore prepare a way for God – and for Jesus – to come into our hearts.

We can't properly prepare unless we know in our hearts that we are expectant (pregnant) that we both want and expect God to come into our lives (just in the same way a mother knows that she is going to have a baby, and so prepares for the baby that she is expecting).

The fourth Sunday in Advent reminds us that Christmas is now very near **(light fourth candle)**. It reminds us that we should now make sure that we are finally ready and make our last acts of preparation. If we get all this right, and done in good time, then we have a better chance of being ready for Christmas Day itself, for the birth of Christ. If we have prepared properly, we will understand that Christ has a light whose power overshadows all other lights, and that power will enter our hearts and minds.

Aids Needed

Candles, children, Advent wreath, involvement; these are powerful aids for our worship.

N.B. The collects from the Prayer Book used during the first Sunday in Advent corresponds with the theme illustrated by the first candle, the second with the second, etc. This is a powerful method of teaching / aid to learning, and can be used with children of all ages, and adults as well.

Have you got a ladder, vicar?

Drama / Presentation

The four candles for Advent should be placed on or near the Altar or lectern or some other strategic point in the Church where everyone has a good view, and remain unlit for the address. At each section of the talk a different child is invited to light one of the candles. The intensity of the light increases as each candle is lit, pointing us to the fact that the birth is getting closer and closer. The nearness of the Christmas event ... the birth of Jesus ... is now just around the corner.

Visual Aids

A simple set of 'Advent Candles' consisting of metal holders for four candles, angels, bells, etc., can be purchased from many department stores, otherwise a simply decorated board bearing four candles, or even four candles placed at advantageous positions in the Church ... matches, tapers, candle, Bible, children.

Notes The Advent Candle theme can either be used on the first Sunday of Advent or can be used as a basis for four talks during the four Sundays of Advent, lighting one additional candle each week. Families quite often enjoy making their own set of Advent Candles and lighting them during Sunday lunch times at home.

NO 3
THE SEVEN CANDLES OF FAILURE

Theme and Preparation

In an attempt to portray my message, I decided to use seven candles in the shape of a cross in the aisle or choir, held aloft by children, initially alight, and then extinguished one by one. (The seven lights were extinguished one by one as we thought about our various failures.) We remembered that seven human failures were brought before Christ, and that he transformed or changed them. By extinguishing these candles of failure, we created a visual reminder that no matter how often we fail, and no matter in how many different ways, Jesus gives us the chance of new life (and at this point in my narrative the candles were then relit). As we prepare for Christmas, and get ready for the coming of Christ, it is important to look at some of the ways that those who were close to Jesus failed him. He was so often let down by those who were closest to him. Very often we focus on how people have let us down, but we should also focus on the fact that we too fail those around us. It can sometimes be in these same or similar ways that those around Jesus failed him 2000 years ago. As a part of our Advent preparation, we should offer our failures to God, and ask that they be transformed by His love.

Candle 1

James and John failed to see the true nature of the mission of Jesus. They thought that he had been born to be a great hero – a conqueror of the Romans and liberator of the Jews. So, they asked that once he was victorious they could sit one at His right-hand side, and the other at the left-hand side of Jesus. This can be called … the **"being top of the pile"** syndrome … and many of us like to be the most important person around.

Candle 2

The disciple John failed to see that from the very beginning suffering and death was the way of Christ, and if we truly want to be faithful, then as modern disciples we must follow this example that Christ set for us… When John was told by Jesus that giving his own life was what God required of His Son, he said, "Never, that will never be"…

This is **"The not facing the truth of God's call / The Easy Way Out"** syndrome.

Candle 3

This candle represents Judas, who thought he knew better than everybody else, including Jesus. In the end he betrayed Jesus, thinking that that was the way that he would get his own way, and Jesus would be forced to confront the Romans and the Jewish authorities and deal with them in such a way that he would be heralded by the people as their king, and he could then take power ... That can be seen as the **"I'm all right Jack / I know best"** syndrome.

Candle 4

This candle reminds us of the disciple Peter who, when he needed to stand up and be counted, displayed a complete lack of courage. He lacked the staying power to stand by Jesus, and when the going got rough, actually denied Jesus three times. During the trial of Jesus he was accused of being a follower, a disciple, and wasn't prepared to stand up and be counted ... "What, me?" he said. "I don't know the man" (referring to Jesus).

How pathetic ... And how pathetic we all are at times when it comes to standing up for the truth. It can be called **"The insecurity syndrome"** because we don't feel confident enough to stand by the truth when it might be costly to do so.

Candle 5

Pilate was the Governor of Judea; he ruled the land where Jesus was born and lived ... he was a man of great power and authority. Even though he had such great power, he failed to do his duty, and did not ensure that Jesus had protection and the right to a fair trial. He was a man who cared more about retaining his own position than he cared about truth and right and justice, and so he turned his back on Jesus when Jesus needed him most, and simply protected his own position ... it can be called the **"Washing of Hands"** Syndrome.

Candle 6

The sixth candle stands for the criminal who was being crucified alongside Jesus and who taunted Jesus, as they both hung there, dying on their individual Crosses. **"Save yourself and us,"** the criminal taunted. He was a man who was so concerned about himself that he failed to see what he had become ... a real villain, and who because of his crimes had lost his way in life. He also failed to see what Jesus was, and that even at this late moment, if only he had realised that he could still trust Jesus, then as he faced death he might still have been forgiven for all the mistakes that he had made in his life ... This is the **"Me at all Cost"** Syndrome.

Candle 7

This candle stands for the crowd who gathered around the cross, and who jeered at Christ. Sadly, we all 'jeer', we all very often ridicule situations that we discover around us, because often we all fail to recognise the love and the beauty in the people around us. We get carried away by the crowd, and simply echo the commonly held prejudices … This is the **"Safety in Numbers" syndrome**.

I won't put it out! I won't be a failure!

Drama Presentation

At the beginning of the talk seven children should be invited to each light one of the seven candles. The candles are then carried aloft to the crossing in the aisle and held (still aloft) in the shape of a cross. As each of the seven failures is talked about, one of the candles is extinguished, symbolising the fact that each of our failures separates us from Christ, who is the Light of the World, and that through His love for us, Jesus can be the one who lights the path we tread throughout our lives. At the end of the talk, bring the seven candles to the Altar. This simple act symbolises that we should always submit our failures to God. Place the seven candles on or round the Altar, unlit, and then invite everyone present to use a short time of silence to offer our sins and mistakes to God and ask Him to purge us of all our wrongdoings. This is equivalent to asking that using His power and love, our hearts and minds will be cleansed. We then relight the candles, symbolising that God can always be the giver of our redemption … which means the giver of new life.

Visual Aids

Seven children, seven candles, tapers, matches.

NO 4
CHRISTMAS GIFTS

Theme

Why do we give presents to each other?

Do you prefer to give a present or to receive one?

What are the gifts we offer at worship?

What are the gifts we receive from God?

I wonder if you have ever thought about what it means to say that 'We offer our lives to God'? – Presumably, we try to do so through the way that we use our money, and also the way that we use our time, and perhaps most of all, use our special gifts or talents. We also offer our lives symbolically to God as we receive the bread, and the wine, at the Eucharist and beyond that, through the time that we spend on our worship, both through saying our prayers in private, and by joining with others in doing so in Church. As Christians, we come to understand that it is through our giving to others that we make both ourselves and others more complete. Children love gifts, they love giving, they love receiving. Every child will delight in the opportunity to bring a gift to God, a gift to be blessed, a gift to be talked about, a gift to be given away.

Every time we give a present to someone, it is symbolic of God giving himself for us through Jesus. It also represents Jesus giving his life for us on the cross, the most important gift of all. It represents the Church giving itself for the World. (We must deliver the goods!) Every child can be involved in this. Each child can bring their gift to the Altar for a blessing. Every child can deliver a present to someone in need. The Minister himself can bring a gift. Perhaps at Christmas it can be a special item wrapped up in Christmas paper, and moreover it can include Jesus (a picture ... or the Crib figure) at the centre of the parcel.

Drama / Presentation

When the address is about to start, invite all the children to bring their gift and place them on, or near the Altar, or even allow the children to stand around the altar / table and hold up their gifts to be blessed. The Minister should then unwrap his own gift. He can talk about the fact that when Jesus was given to the world by God, he came in a way that no-one could properly see or understand!!

He says he was made to give his gift to God...
and now he wants it back

Visual Aids

A Christmas gift wrapped up with a figure of Jesus inside / at the centre.

Notes

1. If the gifts offered during the Church service are to be sent to hospitals, or Homes for older people, hospices, etc, then letters should be sent before the day of the Service asking permission for the children to visit, and perhaps for them to be accompanied by their teachers and / or parents to deliver these gifts to suitable recipients.

2. A week or two before the Service indicate by letter sent to / given to the whole Church, and especially to parents, the kinds of gifts required. e.g., Toys, Books, Tins of Food etc, asking for the gift to be labelled appropriately, e.g., boy aged 6, girl aged 7, older person etc.

3. Invite all the parents and children to remain in Church at the end of the Service, or else to come back to the Church at another suitable time, to collect a gift to be delivered. Arm them with a card or letter from the members of the Church giving the recipient good wishes for Christmas and explaining where the gift has been sent from.

THE WATCHERS OVER BETHLEHEM

Theme

If during a Service one is able to include simple pieces of drama, then without doubt that quickly and delightfully brings the act of worship to life.

This particular drama is self-explanatory and indicates the Christmas theme extremely well.

Narrator

It is Christmas Eve. A child and her Grandfather sit on a hillside overlooking the town of Bethlehem and they watch people come and go both in its busy streets and into and out of the town.

Child

Look, grandfather, look at those two people coming down the hill into the town with the donkey. They look as if they have been on a long journey. (PAUSE) I wonder where they will stay?

A couple enter the Church, obviously husband and wife, and they move from place to place, trying to find accommodation. Every door they knock at is opened and then closed in their faces. Eventually, they vanish out of the Church door into the darkness. All this is watched closely by the two figures on the hillside, grandfather and grand-daughter.

Child

Grandfather, why did everyone turn the travellers away? Grandfather (PAUSE) Why has it suddenly turned so cold?

I wish the night were warm again. Grandfather, it doesn't seem like Christmas any more.

Grandfather

Down there in the town it isn't Christmas.

Child

But, Grandfather. I thought Christmas happened everywhere.

Grandfather

No, child. I wish that it did. But Christmas only happens where doors are open.

Narrator

This is the key to Christmas. Christmas happens when doors are open … Or in other words, when hearts are open to the needs of others. God is always open to us and to our sharing with Him our own needs. He has opened His door to us, and it is permanently open. Do we accept God's invitation? For accepting this offer means that we understand that it is only where doors are opened that love is shared, only where doors are opened that barriers are taken down and relationships begin!

Never mind the lipstick, Sylvia … I don't think they had lipstick 2000 years ago… Please just knock on the door

Drama / Presentation

This is a very moving sermon slot. The Narrator can be at the Chancel step or the pulpit, the child and grandfather perhaps behind the Altar, or if there is a gallery they can be 'overlooking' the event from there. The husband and wife come through the porch into the Church from outside, moving round the Church, knocking on the end of pews, and eventually vanishing out of the Church again into the darkness.

Visual Aids

Five people dressed up appropriately.

NO 6
THE PEACE AT CHRISTMAS

Theme

Imagine the excitement of the Christmas Midnight Service, with the darkened Church full of people, but dimly lit by candlelight. Then the choir coming to the crossing in the nave, perhaps bearing candles, and then into the silence of the darkness, everyone hears these words being sung in a round by the choir:

"It would be a goodly thing, if all people of the world could live together in Thy peace."

And as the round continues, the choir breaks into four-part harmony and begins to move away from the crossing to the extremities of the Church, sharing the Peace of God (a handshake, a wave, a kiss … COVID permitting) with everyone else as they pass them. This very simple act is a marvellous introit to the Midnight Eucharist, but would also be just as fitting if it were a part of the offertory, or the conclusion … and indeed could be used in a different Christmas service altogether.

Music

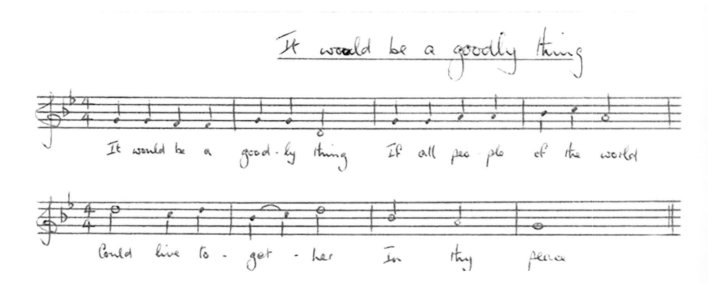

Drama / Presentation

Church choir or other suitable voices to stand at the crossing of the Church, prior to the start of the Service, the Church in darkness if possible. Sing the round through twice in that position, and then as the groups move to the four corners of the Church, the singing becomes pianisimo, all groups fade away on the phrase "In Thy Peace". The singing of the round should be repeated as often as seems appropriate.

Visual Aids

<u>None!</u> Although the choir could carry candles, or perhaps lighted tapers.

It would be a goodly thing ... if you could sing in tune!!

NO 7
GOD'S FAMILY

Theme

The three central characters in the Christmas narrative say so much to us about our own family life:

Joseph

The father of Jesus symbolises the "provider", even though these days both mother and father usually share this task. Even today the father is still quite often the creative one in the family ... creative at least in the sense of being the house builder, using a saw, hammer, bricks, chisel; all these tools and skills that represent the role of the provider. All this reminds us of God our Father the creator, the maker of things, the one who underpins our own lives, and our own family life.

Mary

The mother of Jesus. She is the one who gave birth to new life, the one who shares in the act of creation with the father, the one who usually holds together the family. She is so often the one who makes a home, who shares out the food. What better symbol of motherhood than a loaf of bread?

Jesus

The child reminds us that family life can be greatly enhanced when there are children present. The child's role is to learn, to play, to love, to bring joy and life and laughter to the home. Although there are no records about it in the Bible, we can be sure that Jesus did all that.

These three together, Joseph, Mary and Jesus, remind us that God is our Father, the creator. The Church is our Mother, and holds us together as a Christian Family, and that we, each of us, are one of the children of God, and our task, like that of Jesus, is doing our best to bring life and light to the World.

Drama / Presentation

Before the Service, 'set up' a card table with three candles on it, and place around the card table three chairs. As each of the figures is talked about, invite an appropriate person to come to the table (you will need to arrange this beforehand). Ask them to bring with them an appropriate symbol for the person that they represent …. perhaps a saw or hammer for father, a loaf of bread for mother, toy or books for child, etc. When they get to the table, and have sat down, ask them to light a candle. Then allow each of them perhaps a minute to talk about the object they have brought up, and why it is an important symbol for them. If the service is a Eucharist, ask these same three people to bring up the loaf of bread and a flagon of wine at the Offertory for use during the Communion.

Visual Aids

Folding card table, three people ... man, woman, child, three candles in three place settings, woodwork tools, loaf of bread, flagon of wine, books and toys.

NB. In the light of our modern understanding of sexuality... and of motherhood and fatherhood, this may need to be adapted from the way that it was presented here, but that is not difficult to achieve.

NO 8
COMMUNICATION

There are so many ways that we communicate with each other. We can communicate through our music, painting, theatre and sculpture, and so on. Words… speech is often a poor way of communicating and we are so often misunderstood.

Yet it is important to realise that as we try to communicate with each other and understand each other, and help others to know us more completely, none of the ways identified above are sufficient, or can stand alone; they complement each other. All of them are necessary, and contribute each in their own way to our overall attempt to tell and show others what we think and how we feel. So, it's worth pausing for a moment to think how we communicate with God, and how He communicates with us. Communication, even with God, can be very complicated, and happens in so many different ways. Some obvious examples of understanding what God is telling us might be through very simple things in the world around us, such as flowers or birds or the sky at night. Then through the people in our lives, through prayer, through public worship, through the Spirit of Jesus, and through the Bible. God also communicates in a whole number of different ways. He does so through the beauty of his creation, and perhaps most of all, through our relationships. We ought to spend time every day communicating through our prayers, and every Sunday as we join together with other Christians as a family, to offer to God our praise and our thanksgiving and to listen to His Word. All this, of course, brings us to the supreme way that God has communicated with us. Because of His love for us, He has shown us Himself, and also revealed His true nature, and given us the gift of Jesus.

Who needs words if you can growl?

Drama / Presentation

As each of the methods of communication is talked about in your address, use one or all of the following illustrations:

For smell: ask someone to come forward and identify the mystery smell, and then a second person another different smell, and perhaps even a third.

For touch: two people to come up and hold hands and then take a firm grip of each other. Ask for volunteers – be careful whom you choose, and make sure that you avoid any embarrassment! Talk about the ways in which we hold hands, and what this can symbolise.

For speech / language: again, two people, perhaps one to be given a candle or a thimble, and that person be asked to describe it, without using its name, and without allowing the congregation to see it.

You can perhaps try describing some music of your choice, or a painting that speaks to you. You can try describing any of these and asking the congregation to try to identify what you are describing. It is not easy and demonstrates the limitations of words themselves (a bit like charades!!)

Visual Aids

(For smell) A bag with bacon inside, or cheese rubbed into a cloth.
(For word description) A thimble, a cassette player or a painting.

Theme

So many of us find it difficult to communicate effectively! Sadly, we often limit our method of communication to the spoken word. It can be a most inadequate way of trying to communicate. There are so many other ways possible, and very often they are better ways.

<u>**First – Smell:**</u> It is so easy to invite children to come and identify an object in a bag by smelling it. You will be surprised at how often they get it wrong!!

<u>**Second – Touch:**</u> Touch is so important to us. For example, two people holding hands can show to each other security and strength. A tight grip of the hands says, "I'll look after you", or "don't be afraid" or even obversely

"I am afraid, please don't let go."

Third – Speech: Words can be so difficult; the same words often mean different things to different people. Misinterpretation can lead to unexpected consequences too. Games can be played to illustrate this. For example, a child can be asked to come out to the front of the Church, and then a word whispered to the child, and the child asked to describe it without using the word. Try, for example, the word "cow".

Fourth – A LOOK

A look can say it all … eg. the way two people who are in love don't need to say a word… their faces say it all when they look at each other.

You can tell from their faces exactly what they are thinking!!!

NO 9
PASS THE PARCEL

Theme

We all know how much children love games! How they love parties! Perhaps the most commonly played game at any party is "Pass the Parcel". We use the same game from time to time in Church, and every time it has been used the children have been absolutely delighted. A parcel is made up before the Service starts, usually consisting of four layers of wrapping paper with four gifts. Before the start of one of the hymns, the parcel is given to a member of the congregation / or choir and passed round the congregation for as long as the verse of the hymn is being sung. At the end of the verse, the person holding the parcel brings it out to the Chancel step and unwraps it and the Minister talks about the object inside.

Possible objects inside the parcel … a candle, a sprig of holly, a Bible, a stamp, but could include a coin, a pen, a crib figure, etc. At the end of each verse, the next layer of wrapping paper should be removed.

1. First, a Candle

Why a Candle? As Christians, we believe that Jesus is the Light of the World – Jesus gives light and life to the darkest places. After the Service, the candle is given to the person who discovered it inside the parcel for them to take home to put on, or near, the Christmas cake, so that it can be a constant reminder to that person, and their family, that Jesus lights their lives, and gives us the light of God which shows us how to live.

Now the hymn starts again, and during Verse 2 of the hymn the parcel is passed again, and when the music stops again the person holding the parcel takes off the next layer to find the next hidden object inside.

2. A Sprig of Holly

There are three things about holly that strike us as important:
(1) Firstly, it is evergreen. That reminds us of the eternal love of God.
(2) Secondly, it bears red berries, symbolising the blood of Jesus shed for us.
(3) Thirdly, the leaves have prickles, reminding us that any sacrifice can be painful, and also that if we are thoughtless we can easily give pain to others.

I said put some holly inside ... not mistletoe

Now the hymn starts again, and during Verse 3 of the hymn the parcel is passed again, and when the music stops again the next layer of wrapping paper is removed to find the next hidden object.

3. The Bible (or a gospel)

Why a Bible? Well, because if as Christians we wish to go on learning about God and Jesus, we need to go on reading the Bible. The Bible is the word of God, and by reading it we find out more about both Jesus and God, and this process should continue throughout our lives.

Now the hymn starts again, and during Verse 4 of the hymn the parcel is passed around again, and when the music stops again the unwrapping continues to find the next hidden object.

4. A Stamp

Why on earth a stamp? Well, what is the story of Jesus about? It is about the love of God for you, for me, for everyone in the whole world ... and the best way of experiencing God's love is by sharing that love with each other. Christmas is a time when many of us give and receive love. When we have received presents, the very least we can do is to give back our love and our appreciation by writing to say "Thank You". Not a bad idea to do it today, otherwise it can get put off and off and off ... And sometimes it ends up by never being done at all. Take the stamp home and use it today!! (The person leading the worship can also perhaps explain that any child present might have been the one who did the final unwrapping and who would then have read the message (... and so give everyone / every child in Church, a stamp as if they had been the one unwrapping the parcel!!) and let them take the stamp home and use it on an envelope with a letter inside (written as a thank you note today).

"That's lovely, William ... But I said put six presents inside... not just one for yourself"

Drama/Presentation

At the beginning of the talk, give the parcel to a member of the congregration, If you wish, more than one parcel can be used. Divide the congregation into suitable sections if there is a large attendance. At the start of the chosen hymn or carol, the parcels are passed round in the normal manner as they would be at a party. At the end of the 1st verse, the person / child holding the parcel brings it to the Chancel step and unwraps if to find the first gift. This is held high and shown to the congregation and talked about. Etc.

Visual Aids

Either one, or a number of parcels identical with four layers of wrapping.

The gifts that I used were (from the centre outwards)
1. Postage Stamp for 1st class post
2. Copy of the Gospel (paperback versions of single gospels are easily available)
3. Holly with berries
4. A Candle

Other possibilities: Christmas card, bar of chocolate, coin, crib figure, a pen.

NO 10
HAPPY BIRTHDAY, JESUS

Theme

I would think that at every birthday party that is held anywhere in the world, those who are present will sing Happy Birthday. I imagine that it is the one thing that every child identifies most of all with birthdays, it is the one thing that brings the meaning of the day, and why the party is being held at all, most clearly home to them.

So … whose birthday is it on Christmas Day? Why not a Birthday Cake? Why not light the candles and blow them out? Why not sing Happy Birthday and eat the cake after the Service? It brings home to the children that it is the birthday of Jesus, and that is what we have come together to celebrate … We are having a 'Worship' party in his honour.

Drama / Presentation

Give tapers to a number of children, place the birthday cake on the Altar with a number of candles, e.g. 20 candles – one for every hundred years.

You can ask the children what is the reason that there are 20, and could there be other appropriate choices for the number of candles!

Visual Aids

Cake (Birthday or Christmas), perhaps prepared by one of the congregation, candles, tapers, knife, paper plates, napkins.

<u>**Notes**</u>

You might discover that one of the congregation also has a birthday too on Christmas Day, and would happily share their own cake with Jesus and the congregation. These days most Churches have an area for socialising, but if there is no other suitable area it is advisable to take the cake to the porch to be cut up for distribution. This Service was devised as the introduction to a Christmas party, but can be used on a wide variety of occasions. This short, happy piece can be the best possible introduction to a Christmas Family Service. Sponge cake with icing is the easiest and simplest type of cake for this event.

"Is the Vicar 1,000 years old today?"

AND THE WORD WAS MADE FLESH

Theme

All children love mystery and awe, magic and guessing games. It is not difficult to get hold of 2,200 matches, a small piece of potassium, a bag of lime, some magnesium strip, some sulphur, seven tablets of soap, a sugar sifter full of icing sugar, and a gallon jar of water. Once assembled, one has more or less the chemical ingredients of a human being. These can be distributed among the congregation and brought up one by one as the preacher explains that today something very special is going to be made **(NB. The something special does not include the wood of the matches... just the 'head')**.

As they are brought to the front of the nave (if in a Church) the contents can be put together in a container **(NB. Do not add potassium to water)** and stirred round. The children will have great fun identifying what the different substances are, and even more fun in deciding what they might make when they are put together!! Having got this far, it is quite clear that something is missing. The children might need a bit of prompting, but with help will quickly supply the answer: 'The Spirit of God, or the Spirit of Man'. That is the 'something' that we cannot supply. It should then be explained that that is the bit of "God in us".

Doing all this forcibly demonstrates to us that the birth of Jesus shows that God became man, and that God dwells in each of us. It is the ultimate demonstration that the Word was made flesh, that the Spirit of God is in every human being. This is God's most precious gift to us, and it is what we celebrate on Christmas Day. Then, for the grand finale, imagine the children's delight, the joy on their faces, as a large packing case bursts open and a child jumps out. The incarnation actually happens, the word truly has become flesh.

Drama / Presentation

A local school will supply magnesium and sulphur and potassium. The rest of the aids are quite easily obtained. During the Service, as each item is brought up, talk about each; allow a child to taste the sugar, and another to smell the soap. Drop a tiny piece of potassium into some water (do it with great care, and preferably with tweezers ... and use a very tiny piece, making sure that the level of the water is well below the rim of the glass). Burn the magnesium strip with care, and don't hold it over carpet or anything else inflammable. (You will need a strong flame to set it alight ... so practice beforehand!!) Then as a finale ... the packing case bursts open and the child appears. You have manufactured your very own incarnation.

"So sorry, but I misread the instructions, and haven't brought enough to make what I want to make... I need to ask... has anyone here got 2,199 matches?"

Visual Aids

2,200 matches

Small piece of potassium, bag of lime, magnesium strip, sulphur, seven tablets of soap, sugar sifter, gallon jar of water, taper, matches and a large box / packing case or a suitcase with child safely inside

> **Notes**
>
> Ensure that the box or the suitcase is well ventilated ... the child may well be in there for some time. Magnesium and potassium are both dangerous metals. A local school will supply the magnesium and potassium. Take adequate precautions ... E.g., fireproof floor-coverings, tongs, eye shields etc. For 2,200 matches, simply use a large pack of a dozen boxes to symbolise the quantity.

NB. There will usually be spontaneous applause when eventually, having placed the box in a very prominent position in the Church, the child springs out of the box at the right moment during the talk.

THROWAWAY WRAPPINGS

Theme

All children love receiving gifts, and part of the fun is the unwrapping of them. We all do it in different ways. Some tear off the wrapping paper in a trice (me!!). Others fastidiously undo every knot, cut through every piece of Sellotape, and take forever!! Nevertheless, everyone loves both giving and receiving, and watching others open a gift that they have been given. When we give a gift to someone, we love to make the gift itself look as nice as possible.

During the sermon slot, invite three or four people to come out to wrap up a gift. Provide everything that they are going to need. Tell them to come out and imagine the gift is for someone they love dearly. Father, Mother, Brother, Sister, Friend. Let them choose something from a variety of gifts that you have supplied and then let them wrap it up. Whilst they are doing that, talk about two gifts that are particularly concerned with Christmas, eg. the gift of Jesus as a baby, and the gift to us by the writers of the Gospel stories. Think of the kind of wrappings that they come in; mention the simplicity, the barrenness, the poverty of the stable.

When you talk about the Gospels and the birth narratives, talk about the kind of language the writers use, and their use of vivid detail. You may also go on to talk about the wide variety of languages used in modern translations of the Gospel and so on.

Finally, point out that although they are ultimately thrown away, and can be perceived as having no value, the wrappings do, in fact, make a massive contribution to the way that a gift is both received and valued.

Drama / Presentation

Prepare a table with half a dozen Christmas gifts and wrappers on it. Maybe some of the gifts should be secular, and others religious. Invite three or four people to come out, and let them choose a gift and each of them should wrap it up. Get them to hold up each one in turn and explain (if they can) why they chose that particular gift and wrapping. At the end of the talk, invite those who have wrapped up the gifts to take them away and to give them to someone they love.

Visual Aids

Three or four simple gifts, unwrapped.

Some tissue paper.

Wrapping paper of different qualities, including brown paper.

String, Sellotape.

Stapler, gift tags, gift cards.

"I said help Johnny to choose a gift to wrap... not wrap Johnny"

NO 13
THE CHRISTINGLE

Many will know the Christingle Service; but some may never have led the Service, and so it is worth including here. All children love "doing"; it is part of their nature to be creative, and it is worth reminding them that when they are, they are imitating God. It is Godlike to create. The Christingle ... so simple, and yet so symbolic. We use an orange to represent the round world. It is supported by three cocktail sticks – symbolising the Holy Trinity, God the Creator, Our Father, Jesus his Son, and the Holy Spirit abroad in the world today. These are the three manifestations of God. Use some raisins, sultanas, and cherries to push onto the sticks to symbolise the fruit of the world which has been provided by God. Having cut a neat hole into the top of the orange, there must be a burning candle in the hole – showing the light of Christ standing above the World, and giving light to all around. Then you need some holly which should be stuck into the sides of the orange, representing the eternal nature of God, and the red ribbon representing the blood of Christ, which is wrapped around the 'equator'.

If asked to do so, many will bring an orange to Church on the day of the Christingle Service. Cocktail sticks, sultanas, candles, holly are so easily provided. The Minister can make the first Christingle and light it, but there are many options.

"Please, rector, Jimmy has eaten his orange!"

For example ... members of the congregation can spend a couple of hours the previous day making enough for all the children who will be present, or during the Service those present can be invited to make theirs either where they sit during the Service (time-consuming and messy!!); or better, half a dozen children come out and make one with the Minister, and to do so while he talks, and the rest take the various parts with them when they leave, and make them at home. Or perhaps best and easiest of all, they can all be made before the Service and simply given to all the children present.

Drama / Presentation

Give out the required number of oranges, together with three cocktail sticks per orange, plenty of raisins and cherries, etc. Knives are required to cut a small hole in the top of the orange, but of course they can either be pre-prepared, or use a pointed candle holder which will pierce the orange as it is pushed in. The holly is stuck into the sides of the orange, and finally red ribbon tied round the centre of the orange .

When the talk has ended, the Christingles can be carried in procession through the Church by the children, and then placed on the Altar, showing visually the light of Christ, and then after the Service has finished, they can be taken home to decorate the Christmas dining table.

"Please can I use four cocktail sticks… it keeps falling over"

Visual Aids

Oranges, red ribbons, sprigs of holly, knife, cocktail sticks, damp cloths (to wipe sticky hands). Raisins & sultanas (beware of dried fruit on carpets … they can become very sticky!!).

Notes

The Christingle can be part of the "sermon slot" in a family Eucharist (1 orange), or can be used during part of a Christmas Family Service (6 oranges) or even a service before Christmas Day when the whole congregation is involved (300 oranges).

If you wish to use them, the Church of England Children's Society will provide Orders of Service. But in my experience, it may be better to use this as a basis, and then to modify this to suit the particular occasion and / or venue.

In the Children's Society version, the hymns have words about the Christingle to tunes that everyone knows (e.g. The Holly and the Ivy), so it is well worth getting at least one copy.

Address: Church of England Children's Society, Old Town Hall, Kennington, London SE11 4QD
Tel: 01 234 5678, or simply download from the internet.

NO 14
SPOT THE (UN)INTENTIONAL MISTAKE

Theme

We all know how much children love stories. They especially love to hear stories they know well, and are delighted if they hear them told over and over again.

So very often, when we are reading to our children, and we are in a hurry, we miss out a paragraph, or even a whole page. If we do that, then usually they won't let us get away with it!! They know the stories inside out, and backwards, and if we omit anything, they scream at us to go back and read to them the complete version.

And if we deliberately change a word, or a phrase, they know instantly that we have got it wrong!!

A variant on simply telling the Christmas Story is to tell it and to include a number of mistakes, asking the children to spot these mistakes, and even having a competition between boys or girls, or any other groups present.

So, here's an example:

The Story of the Birth of Jesus

(The mistakes in my version are underlined and in red, but you can, of course, make up your own, and include as many as you wish.)

About three thousand years ago, a carpenter and his wife set out from the town of Nazarene, where they lived, to go to Bethlehem. The carpenter was called Jonathan and his wife Mary. The town where they lived was in Pakistan.

Mary was pregnant. Her baby was due to be born very soon, and Joseph was worried about making the journey. Because it was such a long way, they went by camel train. When they got to Bethlehem, it was quite late, and Joseph went from door to door, trying to find somewhere for them to stay.

Eventually, he went to a <u>fine motel</u>. The innkeeper came to the door and said, "<u>Yes, of course, do come in</u>". "No", he said, "I'm terribly sorry. We are full to bursting, every room is taken, but if you are desperate, you can stay the night in the <u>garage</u>. At least it is dry, and out of the wind, and there is straw to sleep on." Mary and Joseph were very thankful, and they went to the stable and during the night the baby was born, and they called him <u>Justin</u>.

I thought for a moment that it was Mary and Joseph celebrating because they had just been allowed to go into the stable for the night

Mary wrapped baby Jesus in his <u>nappy</u> and put him in the manger. During the night some <u>shop-keepers</u>, who were watching over their <u>stocks by night,</u> came to see the baby Jesus. They had been told of his birth by a <u>telegram</u> sent from <u>Bethlehem Post Office</u>.

A little later, three <u>astronauts</u> appeared from the East. They brought gifts of gold, frankincense and a <u>mirror</u>.

Drama / Presentation

Ask a parent to come out and it can be great fun to mark on a blackboard "Boys and Girls" and keep the score.

This story is aimed at the 4- to 8-year-olds. It can easily be adapted if the congregation has predominantly older children, e.g. if all of them have been confirmed.

For example, "and she laid him in a manger" can become "a place where they keep mangy dogs".

Notes
This type of story can, of course, be adapted to other times of the year: Holy Week, Easter, Ascension, Whitsun. It is a great teaching tool to use with children of all ages.

Visual Aids
Blackboard and chalk.

NO 15
CHRISTMAS DECORATIONS

Theme

1. When were you born?

Ask someone – person X – to bring to Church a birth certificate and then ask them to come to the Chancel step and hold it up and tell the congregation their date of birth.

Now get another member of the congregation – Y (who hasn't been primed to do so, but who was baptised in the Church) to come to the Chancel step. You should then ask, "When was this person, this member of the congregation, born or baptised?"

Have the relevant copy of one of the baptism registers of the Church / parish to hand and ask the person to look up the date in the Baptism register.

Now invite Z to come out, and ask, "When was Z's great-great-grandfather born?"

Ask Z to look in old register. (Brief the person beforehand, i.e. have a copy of the relevant register available.)

Now let's move on to Jesus!!

When was Jesus born?

We do not know. No certificate. No register.

2. So how did Christians choose the birth date? Is it possible that Christians have taken over a pagan festival to celebrate the Birth of Christ, or have we just chosen a date that they think makes some sense?

They could have chosen New Year's Day, Midsummer's Day, But they chose Mid-Winter. This is because it was thought in ancient times that December 24th was the shortest day of the year, and people used to celebrate the lengthening of the days from this day forwards. As Christians took over this festival, this pagan custom was given a new meaning … that God had sent his Son, on the very shortest day, at the darkest time, to bring us His own new light.

3. What can we deduce from other things that we use for Christmas celebrations and as decorations?

a. Ask a child to bring up a piece of <u>holly</u> – make sure that it has some berries.

Holly was used by pagans to show that when we see evergreen trees in Mid-Winter, we remember that this is a reminder that God gave a promise that no matter how bleak things look, life will always continue. (Another similar symbol is the rainbow.) Look at what some Christians did with this idea of evergreen holly: they wrote a well-known Christmas carol – so this point in the Service might be a good time to either read or sing part of the carol "The Holly and the Ivy".

b. Ask someone to bring out some mistletoe … the 'toe' on the host tree or the twig, and which is fed on by the missel thrush. Tell the Scandinavian folktale of <u>Balder</u>, the Sun God, who could not be killed by anything except the mistletoe. So, <u>Loki</u>, the god of evil, tried to kill him by placing an arrow of mistletoe in the hands of the blind god, <u>Hoder</u>. Balder was killed, but then he was brought back to life. The mistletoe promised never to hurt anyone again. Hence it became a symbol of love. So, it became one of the symbols used within our Christmas celebration.

The mistletoe represents the love that Christians should stand for.

At this point, and with some humour, make a comparison between a kiss under the mistletoe (if you can get two volunteers to come and demonstrate? … but not during COVID!!) and the sharing of the Christian kiss of peace. The first might well be described as Eros, the second Agape. Then, in your address, get someone to look up what these two Greek words mean … easy by Google.

4. The Christmas Tree

Ask a child to stand by the Christmas tree. The tradition of having Christmas trees in our home comes from Germany. Boniface, who was out walking in a forest, meets a crowd who, because of their superstition, are about to sacrifice a boy to a mighty oak tree. Boniface defies this superstition and hews down the oak tree, which, to everyone's surprise, survives. (Later, Boniface is made a saint.) As the shocked crowd look at the fallen tree, and its huge stump, they see in the midst of the tangle of roots there is a little spruce fir tree growing. It has a pointed top, and points upwards to heaven. It is also evergreen and symbolises eternal life.

At least 40 other customs are associated with Christmas, and it is very easy to muddle their Christian meaning with the pagan, so we can perhaps do three things with the three decorations that we have looked at ...

Take the Christmas Tree, around which it is traditional to place gifts, and think ...

"What am I giving this Christmas? Not just in terms of wrapped presents, but in terms of how the gifts that I will give represent how I give of myself. Then look at the last verse of "In the Bleak Mid-Winter".

Take the Holly and think about 'the berry as red as any blood' and remember that Jesus said at the Last Supper, "This is my blood – my life blood poured out for you", and focus on this when we all come to share the bread and the wine later in this Communion Service. Finally, now think back to the Mistletoe, and share with someone you do not know in the congregation the "Kiss of Peace", and as you do so, say to them, "Peace to you at Christmas," or similar words of your own choosing.

(Getting to know other Christians is a vital part of our mission or ministry.)

Drama / Presentation

It is assumed that the Church will be full of Christmas decorations – and there will probably be a tree, holly, mistletoe, etc. If not, make sure that they are to hand ... even a 12-inch miniature tree will suffice.

Visual Aids

In addition to the decorations, you will need the current Baptism Register, and a very old Baptism Register. Then you will also need to ask a member of the congregation to bring their birth certificate to Church.

Notes

This is easy for a busy parson to prepare.

The "Kiss of Peace" could be brought in either as a culmination of this Talk / Sermon, or in its usual appointed place in the Communion Service, if the congregation are used to this being included.

NO 16
MAGNESIUM

Theme

The brilliant glare of burning magnesium can be quite frightening and yet, in its normal state, it is grey, dull, difficult to recognise, and totally uninteresting.

Hold up a piece (it usually comes in a roll, so cut off a 6-inch strip) and ask children if they can recognise it. They probably will not. It's Magnesium; So what? Then explain that the same was true of Jesus ... During his lifetime so many failed to recognise him; and even today so many still fail to do so. In life it is absolutely the case that if you fail to recognise something, you probably are not going to use it as you should.

But even if you know what an object or a substance is, and what it is used for, you have got to know how to handle it. Some things can be very dangerous if they are not dealt with properly. Magnesium is dangerous; it should be handled with care using tongs and gloves. It has to be prepared for use. We have to know what to do and be prepared to use it appropriately.

Now burn a small piece of magnesium

Having burnt the magnesium, then continue ... The same is true of God. The same is true of Jesus. Having recognised him as being God's son, we must be prepared to accept this as the truth about him, and then to use this knowledge in the right way. If we do so, it will have a profound impact on our lives, and on the lives of others.

Now burn a big piece ... a long strip (suggest 12 inches)

Then continue ... As you have seen, I have just set fire to the magnesium; which has given a tremendous light and filled the entire Church. God is like that. There is such tremendous power waiting to be liberated, to be used by us all. But first we must recognise God's power and understand that we have to be prepared to handle it properly and carefully. If we do so, the power released can change our life and the lives of others.

Drama / Presentation

Hold up a strip of magnesium for recognition. Hold up gloves and tongs. Talk about preparation and care. Wearing the gloves, burn a short magnesium strip and then repeat with the longer strip.

Visual Aids

Thick old gloves, strips of magnesium, tongs, matches or a lighted taper.

Tapers, solid floor covering, an eye-shield should be worn.

A bucket of water standing by... just in case!

Notes

MAGNESIUM IS VERY DANGEROUS.

Do not light it over soft furnishings.

Always have a bucket of water standing by in case of emergency.

As you burn strips of magnesium, sometimes pieces will break off and fall to the ground, and if it does you can stamp it out very easily.

The local school will almost certainly be able to supply most of the visual aids you need for this.

And, of course, you can ask the Chemistry Teacher from a local school to come and demonstrate it and talk about how magnesium is used in industry.

"Don't you think it would have been better to have dropped the magnesium in the bucket?"

NO 17
FIND THE HIDDEN CHRIST

Theme

Have you ever had a party? Of course you have.

Have you ever had a treasure hunt? Again ... yes, of course.

You will have seen the great delight when children have a treasure hunt at home and race around the house or garden searching for the objects that are hidden and they have been challenged to try to find them.

When the three kings set out on their 'treasure hunt' to search for and find Jesus, they did not know, firstly, where they were going, and then secondly, they had no idea how to get there, and then thirdly, they could not possibly guess what they would find when they arrived ...

It is interesting to try to discover just how hard their task was. Tell the children that an object has been hidden in Church. Who would like to find it? Invite a child, or a group of children, out to the front, and ask that they find what has been hidden.

> **"Go on, then ... try and find it."**
> **"No, I'm not telling you what it is. That is part of the problem.**
> **The Wise Men didn't know what they were looking for... and so nor do you."**
>
> **PAUSE**

If you started with inviting just one child to search, you can, at this stage, add two more children to the search, to mirror the search of the Three Kings.

Give them a couple of minutes ... And then say to them ...

> **"All right, you've failed to find what I have hidden. Well, now I want the whole congregation to search. Yes, I mean everyone. Go on, everyone. Try and find it."**
> **(What chaos!) Go on everyone. Try and find it"**

PAUSE

"I think it is better if I give you a clue. You are looking for the child Jesus out of the crib. Now can you find it?"

PAUSE

"Yes or no, [name of person], you are getting warmer, colder, etc" as necessary.

And now wait until someone discovers it, which they surely will ... eventually.

"Well done! Here it is, here is the baby Jesus. Well done [name of finder] ... set it down. It was just the same for the Three Kings. Without doubt they constantly had to ask, "Is this it?" "Are we there yet?".

Drama / Presentation

Before the congregation arrive, hide an object in Church; for example, the figure of Jesus from the crib. Make sure that it is well hidden ... perhaps put it under a radiator well away from the main part of the nave.

If people don't know what they are looking for, it is very difficult to find it.

and we still cant find it .... whatever we do

That is possibly why the Three Kings stumbled into Herod's palace. Who better to ask than the King of the country? He would be sure to know. He should know everything. As searchers from a foreign land, they needed guidance all the time. We are told in the Bible that is why the star appeared.... To guide them. And yet, amazingly, once they were at the stable, they instantly recognised the child for who he was … THE SON OF GOD. That too is a mystery … How did they do that? ... Why didn't they turn away and go somewhere else to continue their search?

METHOD
Call out a child; tell him or her to find the object
Failure
Add two more children to the search
Failure
Now tell everyone to find the hidden object. If still failure, tell them what they are looking for.

Visual Aids
Object to hide, of course
A child!
Two more
Whole congregation

Notes

Be prepared for chaos when everyone is searching. Also, be prepared just in case the object is found immediately by the first child (though I have never known this to happen!) … and perhaps have a second object hidden, just in case, which hopefully you won't need to disclose.

NB. We have known the Verger to find it before the Service and remove it! So check it is still there just before the Service starts … or better … warn the verger!!

NO 18
THE WISE MEN'S JOURNEY

Theme

Just like the three Kings … the children of the Church are going on a journey to find the baby Jesus.

Invite every child to come to Church with a gift for baby Jesus.

Before the Service starts, choose a 'stable' (a room such as a vestry, the bell-chamber, the boiler house) where Jesus is to be found / discovered. Dress up that place to give a semblance of a stable.

Ask two members of the congregation to be Mary and Joseph for the event, and to dress up for it. If there is a couple with a new addition to their family, they can, of course, include their new child as Jesus … otherwise another baby or even a doll!!

***

Ask another child to be the star, guiding the kings to the stable … This child / teenager will carry a long pole with a small torch or similar light attached to the end and held as high as possible.

Ask three members of the congregation (perhaps three children) to be the three kings and dress up accordingly, and also ask them to bring appropriate gifts that look as much like gold, frankincense and myrrh as possible.

The Church should be in semi-darkness!

At the beginning of the address / the event … ask the star-carrier to come to the choir, followed by the three kings, who will come to the Chancel step. All the children of the Church will form a procession behind the Kings.

With a suitable carol ("We Three Kings"?), the procession can begin its journey.

Tradition has it that they made the journey by camel … but this is not certain, of course …

"If I sit between the two humps it is far too painful, so I've decided to walk"

Perhaps the route might be … down the centre aisle, through the transept, into the porch, around the Church itself (provided that there is a footpath!!) and finally the climbing of the stairs up to the belltower (or wherever Mary and Joseph are hidden) … where the three kings will give their gifts, and then followed by every child who will also present their own gift.

On the way, you can, of course, include as many interludes as appropriate.

For example, the kings can stop off at Herod's a palace you 'create' in the Church or hall, and Herod can summon his advisers to give directions.

When the children have returned to the warmth of the nave, then have a conversation with them about the journey. The following questions might provoke reactions:

Was it easy?
Did they know where they were going?
Did they know what they might find?
Were they anxious that they might get lost?
How helpful was the guiding star?
When they got there, were they made welcome?
Did Mary and Joseph like their gifts?

Did they receive a big thank you?

Was it worth all the trouble of making the journey?

Why did they go at all?

Do they have any idea what will now happen to the baby?

Drama / Presentation

Journey to find Jesus

Visual Aids

Three Kings, suitably attired, and with gifts

The star carrier ... with pole and lamp

Mary and Joseph, with baby (or doll) hidden in the stable

Notes ... The congregation can continue to sing Epiphany carols whilst the drama unfolds, or they can join the searching group and make their own journey of discovery.

(If you prefer that the general congregation are not to be included in the search, then the person leading the worship can give an address (or the organist play a voluntary, etc), which will fill the void during the search ... probably around 5 - 7 minutes will be needed!!) The congregation, of course, will stay in their seats / pews.

SECTION 2
INTRODUCTION

In the section below you will find a number of major Services, each one lasting between 30 and 40 minutes. They are intended to bring us face to face with some important Christian teaching.

They have been created so that they can be used by a wide range of different Christian Groups, such as Youth Groups and Sunday Schools in Church or Church hall, Church Schools, and, of course, State schools, and can take place in Church or in School, or village hall etc.

In this book they are presented as they were used in a Church. They were put together by a group of adults working with me as a team, but in the hope that they would involve many young people. Should you decide to use any of them, they will need adapting to your own situation, and you will probably need to bring together a team of adults/parents/teachers to enable them to happen.

With regard to this last, you may be concerned as to how you will find people willing to help. Don't worry; even if you believe that you are one of the following:

a lone Vicar / Minister with an ultra-cautious P.C.C.

Or a Sunday School Enabler with a stick-in-the-mud Vicar

Or a Religious Education Teacher with an indifferent set of teachers in the Common Room we believe that you will discover that the material here stimulates many individuals into wanting to take part in these productions. Parents will also often be prepared to offer their services as well, so you will find parents offering to make a ten-foot serpent with evil eyes because their daughter is going to be inside!

(See the play "Hell or High Hope" where this occurs.)

Or parents or their friends offering to train eight "Bell Boys" to ring bell changes because they themselves have in the past been campanologists and enjoyed the experience.

(See the play "Ring out Those Bells" to find out more.)

Or you may discover that another group is prepared to create and build a 3m x 2m Jigsaw because they are keen to explain to kids how important the Bible is to them, and especially if their own child (or even the neighbour's child) is Mr Jig the Saw!

(See, in this case, "From God to Man", where astonishing things happen.)

And in another scenario find that someone will volunteer to be a person dressed in black, and singing the bass counter chant, "Evil ... evil ... evil" because they find it so intriguing that they are simply desperate to become involved in the service.

(See "Hell or High Hope" and discover more.)

All of the above have been fabulous experiences for those who have made them happen ... and what is more, these Services have left a personal and vivid impression both on those who have taken part and on so many others.

Some Practical Hints (which you may want to take on board or jettison):

These Services are not intended to be a part of a Family Eucharist.

(However, if you choose to adapt them so that they are, I am sure that that can be done.)

Each one was written to stand on its own as an opportunity for people to experience worship in a different way to normal Sunday Church worship. I have found that one possible good day and time to hold a Service such as these presented here is the Sunday afternoon before Christmas at around 3.30pm, especially if the Service is to be in Church, so that people can arrive before darkness falls. But clearly there are other times that will work equally well, and that might fit your own situation better than my recommendation.

But let me add that I suggest this time and date because:

(a) Most parents are free to come then and share in the Service. There will inevitably be some who are still prevented to do so by work, or other commitments, but most should be able to be available.

You may well want to have a "dress-rehearsal", and experience has shown that is best staged in the morning of the same day. Some of these events / situations can involve perhaps a hundred children;

Is everyone of them going to have a part in the Christmas play?

(a) and when this number are involved, it is important to find a time when virtually all the parents are free to come along. Moreover, if the parents turn up to the dress-rehearsal, they will almost certainly turn up to the Service.

(b) Some of these Services / events can have a major impact if they finish with a lantern-lit procession. This procession can be to a hospital or nursing home, or just round the parish. If you get the timing right, and the darkness falls at just the right moment, then the impact of a long procession by torch-light or lantern-light is spectacular, and will give a huge number of people a great deal of joy and excitement.

If it is a school that is presenting one of these Services, the parents of the children will pack into the school hall or into the local Church on a weekday evening just before the end of term. If possible, fix the date and time as early as possible … perhaps getting it into the diary as early as September. The earlier in the year the date is agreed the better. Make sure that all the parents have the date, together with the five or six dates and times needed for each of the rehearsals.

Donkeys

Younger children love to see a live donkey coming into Church, or school, and then carrying "Mary" to 'Bethlehem'. (See services No's 20 to 23.)

Within a few miles of any Church in England, there will be a smallholding, stables or farm, where there is a donkey. In most cases the owners will be delighted to lend the animal, perhaps seeing it as their contribution to the celebration of 'The coming of Jesus' at Christmas. If they cannot also provide a box for transport, they will almost certainly be able to advise you as to who has one.

If, where the performance is taking place, you have a polished wood floor, put down matting, such as cricket matting, borrowed from the local school. They don't usually play much cricket in December!! Moreover, it is possible for a donkey to slip on the parquet, and even though we have never had a Frank Spencer "Whoopsie" in the Church, it is perhaps sensible to have a bucket and broom and shovel handy just in case!!

Orders of Service

One should have a printed Order of Service. It is such a simple process to create this these days. Every child likes to see their name in print, and every parent revels in the fact that they can show the Order of Service, together with photographs, to grandparents, aunts and uncles and close friends over the following days … or years !!

The Cover

A cover for the Order of Service can be designed by one of the adults helping with the production, but very often some of the children are keen to do it. Sometimes sponsorship – support of financial help – will be given by a local firm. The covers can either be distributed amongst the children for colouring or simply printed in full and glorious technicolour… so easy and cheap these days. (Once one of the schools that we were working with saw the cover that had been designed for "**Hell, or Hope**" and asked for 300 of the covers for the children to colour.)

Children's Names

As I have said above, children love seeing their names in print. It is perhaps best to leave the typing out and printing of the "cast" until the day before the Service takes place. It is not unusual to find that changes occur at the very last minute, and substitutes have to be brought in very quickly!!

Share out the Responsibilities

If you are contemplating doing a production of any one of these Services, there will be a huge amount of work involved! You must not attempt to do it all yourself!! Other adults (and many children) will in any case want to help you, so, if you don't have the time to direct the Service yourself, appoint a "Director" – someone with flair, sensitivity and a loud voice! Almost certainly you are going to need a great many props. Let the director ask someone to take on the task of finding these props (e.g., a telephone in "A

Tale of Four Kings"); and if necessary, another person to help make props or at least create a team to make them (e.g., the "ark" in "From God to Man"); and the director should find another person to be the wardrobe mistress / master and to be responsible for the clothes, and so on. Where there are groups of children in Church, rehearsing or simply waiting for their 'slot' etc, then make sure that at least one adult can to be with each group to keep them occupied.

The more you do this, the more orderly it will be, and the more it will become "our" Service and not just "The vicar's or His or Hers". Moreover, you will not be overwhelmed at the huge amount that needs to be done.

They said that they couldn't find a red candle for the centre ... but they should know that it should be white

PYRAMID OF LIGHT (THE BLESSING OF THE CRIB)

Preparation to be done before the Service

If you can do so, borrow some staging from a local school or drama group, and erect the staging at a central point in Church so that it can be seen by everyone present. (Many head teachers will be helpful if asked.)

If staging is not available, it is possible to use tables.

You will need a large quantity of trays. Fill the trays with 2 inches of sand and place on and around the staging. If night lights are going to be used rather than candles,

sand trays are unnecessary.

Arrange an empty crib on the top tier of the staging, and then set up four candle lighting points arranged at strategic points and not very far from the pyramid … perhaps two or three metres away (see plan below).

And place one large candle in a candlestick behind the crib.

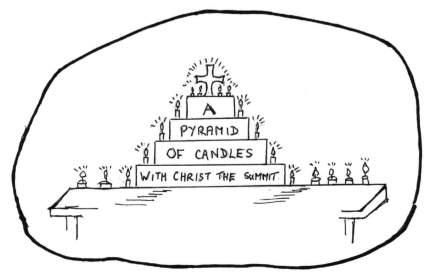

In the plan below:

• A, B, C, D are candle/night light lighting and distribution points. At each point you will need to have tapers, matches, night light/candles.

Preparation before the Service
If necessary, borrow the staging. Then erect it at a central point in the Church.

Fill trays with sand, place the staging around crib. Arrange candles at distribution points together with tapers and matches.

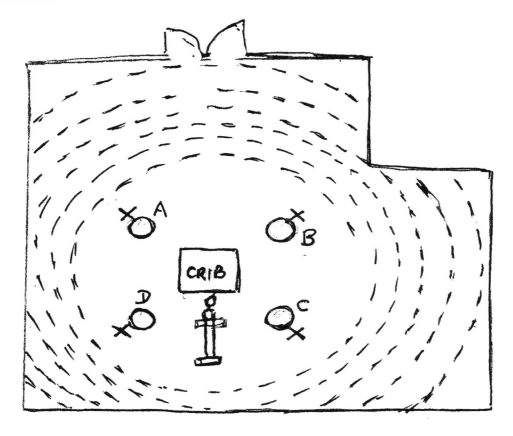

If chairs are available, then seating should be arranged in circles with the pyramid at the focal point. (or as near as possible… e.g., you might find a pillar is in the way).

Place a large / long candle on a tall candlestick behind crib (perhaps use the Pascal Candle, which will give a powerful effect).

Drama / Presentation

Either before or during an early part of the Service, distribute amongst the congregation all the figures to be placed in and around the crib.

Then, whilst the story of the birth of Jesus is being read or told (told is better, and can be done as a combination of Luke's and Matthew's narrative), invite each of the children holding a crib figure to come to the crib and place them into and around the crib in the place where they would be expected to be found.

The usual order of bringing up the figures will be:

Animals, Manger, Mary, Joseph, Jesus (having placed Jesus into the crib and then ask someone to come and light the candle behind crib), then the Shepherds, and finally the Wise Men.

As the children place the figures into and around the crib, invite them to remain near to the crib for the Prayer of Blessing of the Crib.

After the second carol has been sung, invite four fathers or mothers (or four servers) to come to the candle distribution points. Give to each of them a lighted taper.

Every child then comes forward, is given a lighted candle or night light which they place around the crib. Have some adults available to 'guide' the children as to where the candles should be placed. Once they have placed their candle, they should remain at or around the pyramid that holds the crib at its centre.

A pyramid of light is then built around the crib, with the crib as the focus. The effect is truly wonderful.

Lights Out

After the prayers and blessing, the lights should be turned out either in the whole Church, or in the vicinity of the crib. Then invite the children to sing one or two carols ... "Away in a Manger", "Once in Royal David's City", "Little Jesus", etc. When the Service has ended and before people leave, allow photographs (it makes a spectacular diorama) and then as people make their way out of the Church at the end of the Service, do make sure that the lights have been put back on, especially near the main exit.

Order of Service

1. Welcome to families. Distribution of Crib figures to some of the children at the Service
2. Carol
3. Opening prayer
4. Telling the story of the Birth of Jesus (several readers can share the telling of the story) with figures being brought out and placed at the crib
5. Blessing of the Crib

    Prayers of Blessing are found in many books of prayer, but it is very easy to create your own. Perhaps ask the children to write a prayer of blessing, possibly on these lines:

    "Bless, O Father, this Holy Crib, may all who see it, feel the wonder of your gift of love to us at Christmastime. We pray this through Jesus Christ, who was born for us as a babe in Bethlehem, and who is our Lord. Amen."

6. Carol   "Little Jesus Sweetly Sleep" (Rocking carol)

    All children now come forward, take a lighted candle and place it at the crib

        As they do so, each child can say, "Thank you, Father, for the gift of

        Jesus" (or any simple prayer of their own making)

7. Lights Out
8. Carol by the candlelight of the pyramid of candles ("Away in a Manger", "Once in Royal David's City")
9. Prayers by Candlelight

    (1) For the gift of Jesus

    (2) For our families and friends at Christmastime

    (3) for all those in need this Christmas

10. Blessing

Visual Aids

Staging, borrowed from the local school or drama group. Crib and set of crib figures.

Ensure that there are enough candles / night lights (enough for each child) and also some tapers. Candles in star holders can be purchased from Belita Candles. Alternatively, use votive candles and trays of sand. The sand must be at least 3cms / 2 inches deep.

Notes

Because of its popularity, I have had to repeat this Service at both 4pm and 5pm on Christmas Eve. It is intended as the last thing to do by the very young before hanging up their stockings.** It can be seen as an act of prayer and thanksgiving. We use two different cribs at the two Services. The first is taken to a table by the Christmas Tree near the door. The second is eventually placed on a table by the lady chapel door. They both remain *in situ* until Epiphany (Twelfth Night).

** We have also invited the children to bring their stockings to be blessed during the Service and then take them home and hang them up.

NO 20
CHRISTMAS ROUND THE WORLD

1. A number of local schools were invited to explore the theme "Christmas round the world". Each of them selected a country (their own choice) and different classes were invited to take part in a project which displays some of the many Christmas traditions in the country chosen.

2. The date or final Service was fixed at the outset. I would suggest a weekday either in school time or early evening, just before end of term.

3. Three of four days before the Service happens, each school comes to Church to set up their display about the traditions of Christmas in the country of their choice.

N.B. It is essential that these visits are carefully planned, so that the groups from different schools are not 'colliding' with each other or are conflicting with other events that are happening in the Church.

4. Then, during the Service itself, each school or group is given a five-minute slot when they "present" Christmas from the country of their choice. This presentation might include Carols, costumes, stories, reading, poems, mime, dancing, folklore etc.

(See suggested order of service)

5. The displays are then left in Church for the duration of the Christmas Festival period … perhaps mid-December to Epiphany, January 6th (or thereabouts)

6. The order of service MUST be decided well beforehand and both agreed with and circulated to each of the schools / groups concerned. The order should include all carols to be sung, prayers to be shared etc. In addition …

N.B. Invite each of the schools to compile a prayer and then a student or a member of staff to lead this prayer (maximum length of 20-30 seconds).

Order of Service for Christmas around the World

1. Welcome and Bidding Prayer
2. Carol (The word "Carol" should be interpreted as meaning a Christmas Hymn or song, and is to be sung by all those present)
3. Presentation by School 1
4. next ... School 2
5. Carol
6. School 3
7. School 4
8. Carol
9. School 5
10. Talk / Address (suggested theme: "The Universal Christ")

    Christ came for all the world... not just our country... or even just our continent.

    For example, you can show different pictures of baby Jesus (or as an adult) painted by Africans, Indians, South Americans, Europeans, Asians etc, demonstrating that very often every nation adopts Jesus as one of their own people.
11. Prayers

    Someone from each of the schools contributes one of the prayers in the Service (20 to 30 seconds x 5), and and then everyone joins in saying together 'The Lord's Prayer'.
12. Final Carol
13. Blessing

Notes

This Service could be adapted in many ways

1. It could be performed by just one school, with each year group of the school taking a country, or certain individual classes could be asked to choose a country, and the final Service could take place in the school hall. If it is in the local Church, remember that it is easier to fit more parents into the average-sized Church, but please note the journey there may be cold and wet, especially if the children have to walk from school, so perhaps think about the distance involved ... or consider the possibility of arranging transport.
2. Sunday School groups, youth groups, confirmation classes, etc, could equally well be the groups concerned.

N.B. It is important to limit the number of groups to 5 maximum, and the total number of children to about half the capacity of the Church, to allow parents and friends to share in the final act of worship. Give plenty of warning re the date of the Service. For a school to be involved in a project of this sort, the staff would need to know at least two months ahead, and actually the earlier the better. If it is to be at the end of the Christmas term, then arrangements need to be begun in early October, which is well before half-term.

NO 21
A TALE OF FOUR KINGS

This Service requires more preparation than any of the other Nativity Services which follow. Its "bite" comes from the two telephone dramas "No Room in the Ward" and "The Fourth King".

The Service is exactly as produced in my own Church, and so each of the dramas may need a little adaptation.

ORDER OF SERVICE

Hymn 181
"O Little Town of Bethlehem" (everyone)
(There will be an Offertory during this opening hymn)

Vicar asks all to sit

The Coming of John the Baptist

Narrator from the pulpit

a) To begin at the beginning; Our story starts a long, long time ago. Let us go back beyond the latest Christmas pop-song, way back before Bing Crosby was dreaming of a White Christmas, beyond Christmas cards, Christmas stockings, Christmas presents, Christmas carols. In fact, way back beyond Christmas itself…. To an old, old priest called Zechariah, who worked in the temple in Jerusalem. He was soon due to retire from temple duties, and because of this he was about to perform the most important job of his life; he was going to enter the innermost sanctuary of the temple, and whilst he was there, he was going to be allowed to burn some incense. I will let St Luke continue the story … (and as the story is read from the lectern, Zechariah enters from the vestry door and lights and burns incense on the high altar).

The next section of St Luke's gospel is read from the lectern.

The Angel Gabriel appears from the transcept and says …

"Do not be afraid, Zechariah; your prayer has been heard; your wife Elizabeth is going to give birth to a Boy, and you will give him the name 'John.' Your heart will be full of joy, and many people across the whole world will be glad that he was born; for he will be a great person in the eyes of the Lord, and it will be seen that he was born in order to proclaim the birth of the Saviour of the world.

St Luke says … Zechariah said to the angel

Zechariah says
How can this be true?
I am an old man, and my wife is also well on in years, and past the age of having a child.

And the Angel replies
I am Gabriel the Archangel; I stand at God's right hand, and he has sent me to you to bring you this good news. But now listen to me. From this very moment, you will lose your powers of speech and will be dumb – you will remain totally silent – until the day when these things happen. This is happening as a punishment because you have not believed me, though when the time comes, you are going to discover that my words are to be proved true.

Narrator (as Gabriel goes to Lady Chapel and Zechariah, because he is now deaf and dumb, and cannot speak, writes 'something' on a board nearby in the nave)

And so it happened exactly as the angel had told him. The old man was struck dumb until his baby John was born. When the child was born, Elizabeth, his wife, was going to call the babe "Zechariah" after his father, but the old man, still unable to speak, wrote "His name is John, we must call him John "and after this, God gave Zechariah his voice back, and the first thing that he did was to give thanks to God.

Zechariah says – Blessed be the Lord God of Israel, for he has visited and redeemed his people.

3. The Annunciation

The Narrator again reads
But meanwhile, the Angel Gabriel was working overtime. He visited another person; not an old man, but a beautiful young girl called Mary.

Let's ask St Luke to continue the story:

St Luke reads …
In the sixth month, the Angel Gabriel was sent from God to a town in Galilee called Nazareth, with a message for a girl betrothed to a man named Joseph, a descendant of David. The girl's name was Mary.

The angel went in and said to her –

Angel says …
"Greetings, most favoured one: The Lord is with you."

St Luke reads –
But she was deeply troubled by what he said and wondered what this greeting might mean.

Then the Angel said to her
"Do not be afraid, Mary, for God has been gracious to you. You shall conceive, and bear a son, and you shall give him the name 'Jesus'. He will be great; he will bear the title 'Son of God Most High'. The Lord will give him the throne of his ancestor David, and he will be king over Israel for ever; his reign shall never end.

Mary says – "How can this be when I have no husband?"

The angel says "The Holy Spirit will come upon you, and the power of the most high will overshadow you and for that reason the holy child to be born will be known as the 'Son of God'. Moreover, your kinswoman, your cousin Elizabeth, has herself conceived a son in her old age; and she who is reputed to be barren is now in her sixth month and will bear a child, for God's promises can never fail.

Mary says –   "Here am I. I am the Lord's servant.
                As you have spoken, so be it."

Luke says –   Then the Angel left her.

4. The Visitation
Mary runs to Elizabeth. Mary kneels.

Narrator says
There were no antenatal clinics in those days, so Mary rushed over to see her cousin Elizabeth and share all the joys and fears that mothers-to-be have. When they met, Mary was so full of joy that she knelt as her soul overflowed into words.

Vicar says

Here we will all join with Mary in saying those same words. Let us express our joy at the coming of the Lord by all saying together the Magnificat.

(The Magnificat is said)

5. The Birth

Vicar says – We shall now sing verses 1, 2 and 3 of the carol

"Once in Royal David's City" will be sung

The choir will sing verses 1 and 2, the congregation will sing the third verse only

Vicar says

Will you please sit, whilst we listen to a drama which may well give us thought about Christmas then and now.

This little drama is called "No Room in the Ward"

Harassed man appears from vestry in a dressing gown, picks up phone and dials, and says ...

"Hello, hello, is that the General Hospital? The Maternity Ward, please. Engaged? What on earth do you mean? This is urgent ... urgent, I tell you. Sorry, I am sorry. I am a bit on edge, you see. Our baby's due at any moment. My wife is ... What?

I am through? Oh, thanks. Hello, hello, can I speak to the sister-in-charge, please? She is not on duty? What a fine time! Who am I speaking to, then?

Nurse Mayfield? Well, Nurse, perhaps you can help me. I think my wife, Mrs Mary Carpenter, is about to give birth to our child. Can you send an ambulance for her?

Has she been registered? Of course she has. No. I know she is not due to come in yet, but I think she ought to come in now. What on earth do I pay the National Health Service for? You don't think you've got a spare bed? What on earth do you mean? And you don't think that you can send an ambulance ... Now, Nurse, what is this world coming to? A baby's due; there's no ambulance, no bed, no Sister-in-charge, the telephone is engaged when I pick it up, and you say that you will go and investigate? Oh, thanks.

PAUSE

And now you are saying 'come tomorrow'. What … tomorrow? Why that is Christmas Day, Nurse – yes, of course … and a happy one to you.

But can the ambulance come to fetch her now, please?

Look, I have read accounts of Christmas Day in hospital. Not many staff around.

Have I ever read what, Nurse? St Luke Chapter 2?! Yes, I did, as a kid, years ago.

Pretty, pretty Christmas stuff. But what has that got to do with now? You are joking … You say that I should read it while you're finding a bed for my wife. Me … read it … now? Don't be rediculous … but OK. Anything for you, Nurse."

Puts phone down and goes to Vestry.

St Luke reads

In those days, a decree was issued by the Emperor Augustus for a general registration throughout the Roman world. This was when Joseph and Mary went to Bethlehem for the registration, which was the first of its kind. It took place when Quirinius was Governor of Syria. For this purpose, everyone made his way to his own town; and so, Joseph and Mary went up to Judaea from the town of Nazareth in Galilee, to be registered at the city of David called Bethlehem; because he was of the house of David by descent; and with him went Mary, who was betrothed to him. She was pregnant and, while they were there, the time came for her child to be born, and she gave birth to a son, her first-born. She wrapped him round, and laid him in a manger, because there was no room for them to lodge in the house.

(Joseph and Mary come up the aisle with Joseph leading a donkey. They knock at a door. The Innkeeper opens the door, shakes his head, throws up his hands in horror, but, seeing Mary's condition, leads them to the Chancel & strews straw all over the floor for them to lie on.)

"Little Donkey"   **EVERYONE SINGS this carol, but remains SEATED**

1   Little donkey, little donkey
     On the dusty road
     Got to keep on plodding onwards
     With your precious load

2   Been a long time, little donkey
Through the winter's night
Do not give up now, little donkey
Bethlehem's in sight

3   Ring out those bells tonight
Bethlehem, Bethlehem.
Follow that star tonight
Bethlehem, Bethlehem.

4   Little donkey, little donkey
Had a heavy day
Little donkey, carry Mary
Safely on her way
Little donkey, carry Mary
Safely on her way

No Room in the Ward – Conclusion

The Man appears again from the vestry, picks up telephone and **says**

It doesnt look like the vicar, but it sounds like him!

"Hello, Nurse. You have got a bed. Oh, marvellous.

Thanks. Look, we really must fix transport for my wife to come into the hospital. Yes, yes, I will pay for a taxi after what I've just read in the Bible.

Yes, Nurse, I read what you suggested, and I am sorry for what I said. Honestly, I can't comprehend what happened then almost 2000 years ago! No doctor; no nurse; no gas and air; no hot water even. What a fantastic birth. Seems almost impossible.

You say there was one thing then the same as now? What was that? Love?

Oh, I see what you mean. Yes, there was God's love … it was there all the time.

Oh, Nurse, thank you very much – and a Happy Christmas." (Hangs up.)

"Away in a Manger"

The children sing verses 1 and 2 unaccompanied

6. The Christmas Prayer

Vicar says
Before starting our Christmas Prayer, please will you turn to "O Come all ye Faithful" in our songbooks. It is customary to sing the last verse of "O Come all ye Faithful" on Christmas morning only. But it makes a wonderful prayer of adoration at any time, and today we shall use it as such, with slightly changed words.

So, let us pray together.

O God, as we approach Christmas, we praise and thank you for sending your Son to us – to tell us of your love and to give us hope for evermore.

We shall express our thanks and adoration by saying together the last verse of "O Come all ye Faithful".

Yea, Lord, we greet Thee,
Born on Christmas morning,
Jesus, to Thee be glory given;
Word of the Father, Now in flesh appearing;
Come let us adore Him, Christ the Lord. **Amen**

How the Shepherds came to the stable

Vicar says
We shall now sing **"While Shepherds Watched their Flocks by Night"**.

Narrator
Now, in the same district, there were shepherds out in the fields, keeping watch over their flock, when suddenly there stood before them an angel of the Lord, and the splendour of the Lord shone round them. They were terror-struck, but the angel said, "Do not be afraid; I have good news for you: there is great joy coming to the whole people. Today, in the city of David a deliverer has been born to you – the Messiah, the Lord. And this is your sign; you will find a baby lying all wrapped up in a manger."

And at once there was with the angel, a great company of the heavenly host, singing the praises of God: "Glory to God in the highest heaven,

And on earth his peace for men on whom his favour rests."

After the angels had left them and gone back to heaven, the shepherds said to one another, "Come, we must go straight to Bethlehem and see this thing that has happened, which the Lord has just made known to us." So they went with all speed and found their way to Mary and Joseph in the stable; and the babe was there, lying in the manger".

"Mary' s Boy Child"

Vicar says
In this next song, solos will be sung by members of the Choir. Will the Congregation please join in the Refrain after every verse:

    Hark, now hear the angels sing
    A new King, born today
    And man will live for evermore
    Because of Christmas Day.

Trumpets sound and angels sing,
Listen to what they say,
That man shall live for evermore,
Because of Christmas Day.

(During the singing, the shepherds and angels gather round the manger in a tableau.)

The Fourth King

The narrator

Now when Jesus was born in Bethlehem of Judaea in the days of Herod the King, behold wise men from the East came to Jerusalem, saying,

"Where is he who has been born King of the Jews? For we have seen his star in the East and have come to worship him."

When Herod heard this, he was troubled, and all Jerusalem with him; and assembling all the chief priests and scribes of the people, he enquired of them where the Christ was to be born. They told him, in Bethlehem of Judaea; for it is written by the prophet: "And you O Bethlehem, in the land of Judah, are by no means least among the rulers of Judah; for from you shall come a ruler who will govern my people Israel."

Vicar says

At this point we have another interlude to listen to a telephone monologue.
The scene is the local Information Office down by the market.
Sitting at his desk there is a languid young man, feet on desk, ashtray full of stubs. Phone rings.

Languid young man

Hello, The Information Office. Can we help you?
You want somewhere locally to stay this Christmas?
Look, all the hotels are full; there is no room anywhere.

Tell you what. I know of a B & B in Burlington Street. It is at Number 113.
B. J King is the name of the owner. Do you know Burlington Street?
You have got a map on your iPhone? Oh, fine.
Hope you have some luck when you get there, and a Happy Christmas to you!
(Puts down the phone and sings to himself a Christmas pop song; then shouts to someone offstage)

(shouts to some-one offstage)

Hey Jack! I've run out of fags. Got any. King-size only? They will do.
I will pay you back at Christmas. You're gonna give me a cellophane-wrapped, hygienically-boxed, cancer-impregnated gift of king-size cigarettes.

(phone rings again)

Hello, Information Office. Mick at your service.
Yes, Sir! You are trying to find a place called "The Oddies"; you've met a splendid crowd who go there?
Ha. Yes! You must have met me and all my friends there – only the best go to the Oddies.

Real name is "Oddfellows' Arms" – easiest way to get to it is up Queen's Road, then left into King's Road; past the Church and it is about 200 yards down on the left.
Not at all, delighted to help. Maybe see you there?

(Rings off, then says to himself)

Funny. B J King, King-size; Kings Road – all kings.
I will have the bloomin' Sovereign on the telephone any moment!!

(Telephone rings)

"Information Office, Mick at your service –
Your Highness? Good day, Your Highness? Your name? Did you say it is … King Caspar?

(Leaps to attention, still holding phone)

Ah, yes, Your Highness, and you have two chums, I mean companions, and they're Kings as well? I see, your Highness, they are King Balthazar and King Melchior.

Well, what can I do for you, Your Highnesses? How can I help?
You're looking for another King? Aren't three enough? No, we've no other Kings here in this area. You say that this one is just here for a few days, staying locally. I have got copies of the registers of the hotels for the whole Borough. There is no king around here, and, at this time of year, we do not even boast a Beauty Queen.

> You know the name of this King?
> Jesus Christ?
> No, we've no one of that name on our books.

And yet you say that you have talked to some sheep farmers in this area who have met this King. They told you that he isn't easy to find. Well, I would be grateful, Your Highness, if you'd ring me when you've found him. I will then let the local paper know. We would all like to meet this King.

Goodbye, Your Highness. (Hangs up)

Matthew reads
Then Herod summoned these kings secretly and ascertained from them the time the star appeared; and sent them to Bethlehem, saying,
(Herod mimes all this with the kings in the aisle of the Church)

Herod then says
"Go and search diligently for the child, and when you have found him, bring me word as to where he is, that I too may come and worship him."

Narrator
When they had finished listening to King Herod, they went their way; and lo the star which they had seen in the East went before them, till it came to rest over the place where the child was. When they saw the star, they rejoiced with exceeding great joy; and going into the house they saw the child with Mary his Mother, and they fell down and worshipped him.

Then, opening their treasures, they offered him gifts; gold, frankincense and myrrh.

Vicar says
We shall now sing "We Three Kings of Orient Are".
(The Kings bring up gifts in appropriate verses, and solo voices sing appropriate verses. The congregation will only please sing the first and last verses, and the chorus)

Concluding Prayers
Vicar (and others can be invited) says

Let us pray
Today, as we remember that first Christmas, we thank God for this opportunity to worship and adore Our Lord Jesus Christ, as did …

    The Angels
    The Shepherds and
    The Kings from the East.

We pray for all those other families and their friends who, throughout the world, but in different languages, in hot weather as well as in cold, are coming together to worship and give thanks for the birth of Our Lord.

We pray for those who cannot gather round the crib this Christmas, because ...
>they are ill in hospital
>they are ill at home
>they are prevented by political pressure
>or because they have never heard about Christmas
>and do not know its wonderful message.

We end our prayers by saying together the prayer taught us by the man who was once that baby in the crib in Bethlehem:
>"Our Father ..."

And now we end with the Grace:
>"The Grace of Our Lord Jesus Christ ..."

Hymn: "O Come all ye Faithful" – finishing with the final verse.
>(During this hymn, everyone lines up, ready for the lantern-lit procession, in which we go up to the nearby Nursing Home, where we shall sing carols with the residents.)

RING OUT THOSE BELLS

The ideas for this Service were originally put together by a group from the Church congregation. Here the service is reproduced in its entirety. You will see that again it culminated in a lantern-lit procession to the Nursing Home near the Church and was followed by a party.

One of the most important features in this Service is the sharp contrast between the swirl of colour and noise in the 'Summoned by Bells' section and the sudden silence on page 3, which then leads on to the prayer of penitence.

If you can do so, it is so effective to ring bells either inside the Church or from your own Church tower.

"I've forgotten the bells ... shall I clap instead?"

This was a very Special Service held in Church,

which was followed by

A Lantern-lit Procession to nearby Nursing Home

1. THE SERVICE

"RING OUT THOSE BELLS"

a.   Carol for Bells to play
b.   "Ding Dong"
c.   Summoned by Bells
d.   The Sound of Silence
e.   The Story behind the Bells

"God Becomes Man" – to include a live donkey and a human camel or two

2. THE PROCESSION into the Church to the music of "Ding Dong Merrily on High", played on hand bells, during which the offertory was taken.

1.   Ding dong! Merrily on high, in heaven the bells are ringing …

At the end of the carol everyone sits down

Commentator 1
Be still, be silent and listen.
Listen for the sounds of God, for God as He is revealed in man.
Let us move, in Spirit, to Africa and hear how
Christians summon people to Church.
(Children hidden from sight beat tom-toms. This is followed by 15 secs of music from the African Mass "Missa Luba")

Commentator 2
Be still, be silent and listen.
Listen for the sounds of God, for God as He is revealed in man.
Let us move, in Spirit, to the South Seas and hear how Christians summon people to Church.
(A young girl, again hidden from sight, blows into a conch shell)

Commentator 3
Be still, be silent and listen.
Listen for the sounds of God
for God as He is revealed in man.
Let us move, in Spirit, to different places of the world to hear how Christians are summoned by bells.

Narrator
In Austria, the farmer in the mountains opens the wooden window of his house and hears, far below in the valley, the steady rhythmic note of the one bell in his Catholic Church, summoning him to worship. Taking his toboggan, the Austrian equivalent to a bike, he sets off for his Church.
        (If possible, one of the congregation, in Tyrolean dress, 'glides' through the Church, pulling a real toboggan)
(Someone – again hidden – plays one low note on deep chime bar.)

In India, where drought has brought poverty to many villages, young girls put on their best sari, and to the summons of the small chime of their Church bell, leave home for worship in the Church of South India.
    (A girl, who is resplendently decked in a sari, walks down the nave and then through the transcept. Someone hidden plays one high note on small chime bar.)

In Canada, where there is little of the kind of poverty that there is in India, through the cold still dry air, the bells of the United Church proudly proclaim their summons to worship. The policeman – a Mountie, still on his horse, and still on duty – listens and prays as his family make their way through the snow to Church.
    (A boy, dressed in red tunic, white gloves, old Scout hat, etc, moves into the aisle and salutes, and a Choir member plays a peal of six on chime bars.)

In Australia, where instead of snow the white is of the foam and surf on Sidney beach at the height of summer, the bells of the Anglican Church reverberate over the beaches, highways, houses, flats; and long before the Service starts, the Church is full, and people sit perspiring in open-neck shirts.
    (A "Family" of 4 come in, walk to the Chancel and sit down in a row, mopping their brows; and again a Choir member plays peal of eight.)

In England, from Lostwithiel to London, from Cathedral and Chapel, bells ring out.
(Perhaps have some bells pealing, on a recording.)

Peals of 6, or 8, or 12 have been heard throughout the ages in country and city, over farm and fen, bells fashioned with loving hands five hundred years ago; bells that have rung to warn of invasion; to celebrate Trafalgar, and Mafeking, and have been heard by all Henry VIII's brides and some of which are still playing today. (Bells on recording again.)

Many of these same bells now summon people to worship; from the boom of the 17-ton Bourdon Bell in St Paul's to our own hand bells ringing changes in this Church, before ringing round the parish during our procession at the end of the Service.

Commentator 4
Be still, be silent and listen.
Listen for the sounds of God.
For God as He is revealed in man.
Let us move, in Spirit, to China and hear how
Christians summon people to Church.

A long SILENCE (20 seconds? Should be enough)

Yes, when there is silence, Christians cannot proclaim the Good News from the rooftops or steeple. Many Christians still live in danger, under threat of persecution for their faith. We have learned this from many Christians living in China. Many Christians in that country are afraid to write letters to their family and friends in other parts of China for fear they will be imprisoned. Already many Christians, including Priests, are in prison, and fear for their lives. The same is true in some Middle Eastern countries.

As we proceed with this story of Christmas; as we go out into the streets later, and proclaim our faith in Carol and Procession, let us remember our brothers in Christ in China and the Middle East. Let us pray that we will have their courage, should we ever find ourselves under a similar persecution. Let us also ask for God's forgiveness when we so often forget them and ignore their plight.

ALL KNEEL AND SING
Lord, have mercy upon us,
Christ, have mercy upon us,
Lord, have mercy upon us.

"GOD BECOMES MAN"

Now, we shall remind ourselves of the story of Christmas, so that, should we ever be in the situation similar to persecuted Christians, we shall be strengthened by the knowledge deep within us, that God came in Christ at Christmas, and that he came for each one of us.

So, let us move back, beyond the time of Joseph and Mary, to their own people in history – the Jews. They had worshipped God for a long time.

They had written their own songs to God, and today we call these songs Psalms. Did they also have bells at that time, 4000 years ago? Maybe they did … or certainly something similar. The Bible certainly hints at bells in some of the psalms, one of which we shall sing.

(We then sang an adaption of Psalm 33 to Gelineau's words and using a modern tune for unaccompanied voices.

Psalm

Leaders	Ring out your joy to the Lord, O you just;
	For praise is fitting for loyal hearts
ALL (again)	Ring out your joy to the Lord, O you just;
	For praise is fitting for loyal hearts
Soprano	By his word, the heavens were made. By
	the breath of his mouth all the stars were made
Bass	He collects the waves of the ocean;
	He stores up the depths of the sea
Soprano	By his word, the earth was made
	He spoke and it came to be
Bass	He commanded; it sprang into being and
	its care he gave to man.
Leaders	So our heart is glad in him
	Because we trust in His holy name
ALL (again)	So our heart is glad in him
	Because we trust in His holy name

Narrator

And so, into this family of Jews, God sends his Son.

Reading: Luke 1 26-31

The Annunciation (ALL SIT)
Read by a member of the congregation

Carol: "Little Donkey"

> Little Donkey, little Donkey, on the dusty road,
> Got to keep on, little donkey, with your precious load.
> Been a long time, little donkey, thro' the winter's night.
> Don't give up now, little donkey, Bethlehem's in sight

During the chorus, Mary mounted on the donkey, and with Joseph leading it, came up the aisle towards the choir / Chancel

Chorus

> Ring out those bells tonight, Bethlehem, Bethlehem.
> Follow the stars tonight, Bethlehem, Bethlehem.
> Little donkey, little donkey, had a heavy day
> Little donkey, carry Mary safely on her way.

Followed by verse 2 and the chorus again

Reading: Luke 2 'The Birth', read by a member of the Scout Movement

Carol: "Mary's Boy Child" (vv 1 and 3)

> Long time ago in Bethlehem,
>   so the Holy Bible says,
> Mary's Boy Child, Jesus Christ,
> was born on Christmas Day.
> (As this is sung, some children dressed as angels join Mary and Joseph at the crib.)

Chorus

> Hark now hear the angels sing, a new king born today
> And man will live for evermore, because of Christmas Day
> Trumpets sound and angels sing, listen to what they say,
> That man will live for evermore, because of Christmas Day.

Followed by verse 2 and the chorus again

Reading: Luke 2 8-16 The shepherds
  Read by a member of the congregation

Carol: **"The First Nowell" (vv I and 2)**

Reading: Matthew 2 1-2, 1-12 The Kings

Carol: **The same carol, "The First Nowell", continues**
  Kings & Camel enter

Prayers … **led by the vicar, with others invited to contribute**

Priest: The Blessing, followed by 'Go in peace and serve the Lord'.

ALL: In the Name of Christ **Amen**

Carol "O Come All Ye Faithful"

The Procession leaves the Church and goes through the streets to a nearby nursing home, and having pre-arranged the visit, and whilst there everyone sings three or four carols with the residents.

NO 23
HELL OR HOPE AT CHRISTMAS

This is undoubtedly the most exciting Christmas Service I have shared in, because it is both Biblical and Theological, and it is also so very dramatic, such that children are completely caught up in it.

a. The Script that we offer has a plan / a diagram at the beginning and the cast and costumes are set out at the end. Children do get excited by this event and even when some decide at the very last moment that they want to be involved, they can easily be incorporated into the different groups and still take part.

b. The Order of Service. Hundreds of these were run off because children really enjoyed colouring them, and a number of primary schools asked for copies.

They can, of course, also be easily printed.

A Dramatic Climax

The aim of the Service is to show that the Bible is still 'alive' today and has a massive impact on many people's lives. In this Service we look at the early part of the Old Testament. Here, though, we show that the Fall of Man, i.e. any individual, or group, or nation, can still happen today, and that the answer to the fall of mankind is the Incarnation and Resurrection, and that this process of dying and being given new life is also still happening today…happening NOW.

All this is demonstrated by a really dramatic moment in the Service …

As Adam and Eve become existentially involved in this world, the "Hell on Earth" cries rise in a crescendo. Eve is shot dead and the Narrator shouts in anguish, "Is there no hope? Has God forgotten man?" and man is shown to be cowed, distraught. Mankind gives up hope.

He's clearly having a blue day … I think he might collapse in agony

The children (and others) all over the Church take up the shout "Hell on Earth". They cry out, they stamp their feet and make "one hell of a loud noise'

    … until …

    Adam, in agony of spirit, collapses over Eve's body.

    Then there is complete SILENCE and into the silence, on single notes (not chords) and played very quietly in a high octave, comes the first line of "Once in Royal David's City".

    It is a fantastic moment.

"HELL OR HOPE – at Christmas"

This Service is one of Drama, Chant, Noise, Movement and Light for as many as up to 150 individuals, or even more should they be available and wish to take part.

Before the Service

a. The Congregation can be greeted on arrival by children who will be delighted to act as ushers.

b. Five minutes before the Service, all the different Groups taking part will move quietly to their places. Group 3, in the central aisle, will stand against the pews, until the readers and the choir / the chorus have passed. Adam and Eve, the Serpent, messengers and innkeeper and wife all move to their places.

> The Angels and the Shepherds will already be in the Lady Chapel.

c. Just prior to the Service beginning, the Crucifer leads the Vicar from the Vestry, collects Readers, Chorus, and Narrator from the Choir Vestry. They all move up the central aisle and go to their places. When they have passed, Group 3 "imprison" themselves in the chairs in the central aisle.

PROLOGUE

Officiant

Good afternoon and welcome. We have come here today to worship, to learn, to listen, to sing, to pray, to act and to enjoy ourselves in the presence of God.

And, because we are in His presence, we shall start with a reading from the Bible. This will be followed by a hymn.

The first reading consists of the first four words of the Bible. One of our younger Church members will read them.

Reader   In the beginning God.

Officiant

"In the beginning God". God before anything or anyone.

That is why our first hymn is not a Christmas carol. It is a hymn of worship to God and God alone.

Hymn ... the congregation sing

Immortal, invisible, God only wise

Officiant   Will you all please sit and listen to our storyteller?

EPOCH 1 – HELL ON EARTH

Narrator

Once upon a time – as all good stories start – there was a man called Adam. (Adam rises slowly from the floor of the Chancel) The Bible tells us that he was a man who lived happily in beautiful surroundings. He lived at peace, and the whole of life was good; for he lived close to God in the Garden of Eden.

Chorus   (a group of children, but also if needed with adults singing)

Man at peace with God in Eden.

   (This continues quietly and steadily as a background rhythm, until the fruit-picking scene)

Narrator

Adam was given a companion, Eve, with whom to share his life. (Eve walks out to join him) And in sharing his life with someone else, Adam became even more happy, joyful and excited. (Adam and Eve hold hands)

And so this story might have ended as many good stories do with Adam and Eve living happily ever after. But this was not to be. For, in their happy existence, Adam and Eve had to obey just one rule, and that was not to eat of the fruit of the tree of knowledge. But a serpent tempted Eve to break that rule. Evil came into their lives because of this serpent.

Counter Chorus   (A second group of children, or also with adults)

Evil, Evil (continuously, harmonising with, in time with …)

"Man at peace with God in Eden"

(Both Chorus and Counter-Chorus build up in volume as the serpent slides towards Eve, until Eve and the serpent touch.)

(As Eve and the serpent touch there is sudden silence and, in this silence, Eve reaches up to the fruit, withdraws her hand … hesitates and reaches up again. She picks the fruit; holds it in her hands and then suddenly takes a bite. She smiles and hands it to Adam, who looks horrified and fascinated. He slowly raises the fruit and bites.)

Musical group

There is immediate noise from the drums and the thunder machine, organ and any other percussion instruments. This dies down to let the Narrator speak.

Narrator

At this moment man 'fell'.... Man became separated from God.

He knew good, but the biting of the apple symbolises that man chose evil ... his own way ... rather than being obedient, and so he was cast out of the Garden of Eden into the big wide world. A world full of dangerous and evil things.

(Adam and Eve walk down the Chancel steps. The serpent slides away. The serpent children the skins that they have been wearing and join one of the Groups immediately.)

Narrator

And what do Adam and Eve find in this world? They find an abundance of man's cruelty to man – they witness their own son, Cain, killing their other son, Abel. And this cruelty is reflected in every part of the world that they visit. They discover hell on earth. And, as we know, this hell on earth still continues today in so many parts of our world ... or should I say God's world?

Chorus

Hell on earth. Hell on earth (many times very loudly. They also stamp their feet and use percussion)
(Adam and Eve then proceed to the first of the five Groups)

Narrator

Adam and Eve encounter five different ways that this hell on earth can be found.

Chorus Sing "Hell on earth. Hell on earth" (quietly and continuously until the first Group join in. Together they sing for four cycles with the group)

Narrator

They discover suffering and pain.

Group 1 Shout the word "PAIN" at the end of each chorus chant.

E.g. "Hell on earth – PAIN". They shout this four or five times. Then they ALL stop.

(Eve suddenly clasps her hand to her leg in agony. Leaning on Adam's shoulder, she limps behind him. They move on to Group 2)

Narrator

Adam and Eve encounter the kind of pain that reminds us of the pain that brings misery to millions today, and Eve finds that she too is permanently maimed. They decide to look further into this hell on earth.

Chorus

Hell on earth ... (as before)

Narrator

They find people who are starving. People who know that and don't care, and on one side of the world, grain rots in barns because some people have so much, while on the other people haven't a crust.

So here's a family who clearly are starving

Group 2

Shout the word "FOOD' – several times.

(Adam and Eve, now holding their stomachs, crawl on towards Group 3. They crawl into the prison made by the circle of chairs.)

Narrator

And so Adam and Eve find themselves maimed and now starving in prison, denied their freedom by the evil of other men. Wherever they look in the world they find people imprisoned. Imprisoned not for the crimes that they have committed, but for no reason at all, except that others, more powerful than they, want them out of the way. There is no logic to this hell on earth.

Chorus

Hell on earth ... (as before)

Narrator

(Adam and Eve struggle for freedom, struggle to escape from the bars and chains.

Group 3

Shout the word "CHAINS" – many times.

Adam and Eve break free, carrying a chair with them.

> (Note that this chair, which is a symbol of captivity in Group 3, now becomes a real chair in Group 4)

Narrator

They escape from prison, only to join the thousands – indeed millions of refugees in the world. Men and women rejected by other men and women. No-one wants them, they are pushed here, sent there, never allowed to settle and lead a decent life. Adam and Eve join the millions who because of their being rejected, have found hell on earth.

Chorus

Hell on earth ... (as before)

Narrator

Adam and Eve relinquish their only possession, which is a chair.

> (Adam puts it down)

Now they are without chair, bed, roof.

They are without shelter.

They have no chance of finding what they need so badly ... which is a home.

Group 4

Shout ... "HOME" ... many times

> (Leaving their chair behind, Adam and Eve move. onto Group 5)

Narrator

Finally, Adam and Eve encounter man' s worst cruelty to man – legalised slaughter of men, women and children under the name of war.

> (From somewhere in Church comes the sound of staccato machine gun fire)

Like so many people, Adam and Eve become involved in war just because they are there in the midst of it, at the wrong time. They find that of everything bad they have met so far, this is the worst hell on earth.

Chorus

Hell on earth … (as before)

Narrator

Suddenly, like so many other innocent victims, Eve is shot dead by a stray bullet. She becomes the latest victim of man hating man. She is killed by war.

Group 5   … "WAR" … Shout many times

(Adam picks up Eve, carries her to the centre of the Nave at the foot of the Chancel steps; lays her down tenderly. He is weeping.)

Narrator

But was Eve really an innocent victim? It was she who started all this. She is like every one of us. Always, it seems, we are a mixture of innocence and guilt.

We are responsible and irresponsible. Our lives are so muddled and complicated. Adam, in his agony of soul, can see no hope, no guidance, no light. Fortuitously, he turns to God.

(Adam turns and flings his arms upwards to the roof of the Chancel and then drops his head in misery)

It is God who has sent him into the world, and now Adam turns back towards God (he turns and faces the other way), but to no avail – he still finds hell on earth.

Chorus

Hell on earth. Hell on earth … (continuously – till Adam collapses – gradually building up in volume)

(Adam then turns to each group in turn. As he points to each of them, they shout their own word till we have

Hell on earth — (sung)

NO FOOD

CHAINS

PAIN

WAR

(All these different words shouted simultaneously by the respective Groups)

Narrator   (shouts in anguish) Is there no hope? Has God forgotten man?

Man is cowed, distraught. He gives up hope.

(Noise increases; children stamp in time)

(At this, Adam falls across the body of Eve and remains there.)

As he touches the floor / bier on which she is laid, the noise (by now enormous) stops, and into the silence, on one single note, comes the organ, or from a single instrument, the first two lines of ...

Organist   Once in Royal David's City

EPOCH 2 – THE BIRTH OF CHRIST

Chorister (Sings)

Once in Royal David's City (1st verse)

All (Sing) (verses 2, 5 and 6)

(During the last three verses, Joseph and Mary come up the Central Aisle, searching for a room. They are met by the Innkeeper, who indicates that he has no room. He does, however, carry out some straw and a manger and places them in front of Adam and Eve. Joseph and Mary settle down on the straw either side of the manger)

Reader – St Luke (Luke 2 vv 1-7)

In those days, a decree was issued by the Emperor Augustus for a general registration throughout the Roman world. This was the first registration of its kind. It took place when Quirinius was Governor of Syria. For this purpose, everyone made his way to his own town. Joseph went up to Judaea from the town of Nazareth in Galilee, to be registered at the city of David called Bethlehem because he was of the house of David by descent; and with him went Mary who was betrothed to him. She was pregnant, and while they were there the time came for her child to be born, and she gave birth to a son, her first born. She wrapped him round, and laid him in a manger, because there was no room for them to lodge in the house.

Did Mary really put Jesus into a crib under the Church altar?

All sing

While shepherds watched
(Shepherds and Angel Gabriel reveal themselves in The Lady Chapel.)

Reader – St Luke (Luke 2 vv 8-16)

Now in the same district there were shepherds out in the fields, keeping watch through the night over their flock, when suddenly there stood before them an angel of the Lord, and the glory of the Lord shone round them. They were terror-struck, but the angel said, "Do not be afraid; I have good news for you: there is great joy coming to all the people of the world. Today in the city of David, a deliverer has been born to you – the Messiah, the Lord. This is the sign given by God; you will find a baby lying all wrapped up, in a manger." Immediately there was with the angel a great company of the heavenly host, singing the praises of God.

"Glory to God in highest heaven, and on earth his peace for all those men and women who follow him." After the angels had left them and gone into heaven, the shepherds said to one another, "Come, we must go straight to Bethlehem and see this thing that has happened, which the Lord has made known to us." So, they went with all speed to the stable and found there Mary and Joseph, and the baby who was lying in the manger.

Chorister and chorus (Sings 1st verse and refrain of "Mary's Boy Child".)

"Long time ago in Bethlehem ...

(During this, the shepherds and angels form a tableau round the crib, angels standing behind, shepherds lying on the ground in front.)

Reader
Matthew Chap 2 vv 1-2 and 9-11

Jesus was born at Bethlehem in Judaea during the reign of Herod. After his birth, kings from the east arrived in Jerusalem, asking, "Where is the child who is born to be king of the Jews? We observed the rising of his star, and we have come to pay him homage". The star which they had seen at its rising in the Eastern sky went ahead of them until it stopped above the place where the child lay. At the sight of the star, they were overjoyed. Entering the house, they saw the child with Mary his mother, and bowed to the ground in homage to him. Then they opened their treasures and offered him gifts: gold, frankincense and myrrh.

All (Sing 1st verse of "We Three Kings of Orient Are")
   (Kings march out to the Central Aisle, halfway down the Nave. They stand in a row.)

Choristers (Sing, in turn, verses 2, 3 and 4)
   (Each king marches up at appropriate verse, bows and makes his gift)

All   (Sing verse 5)

The two Readers (With lighted taper in one hand, large candle in the other, stand above the Nativity scene. They each light a candle and proclaim)

Reader 1
And God said "Let there be light"

Reader 2
And Jesus said "I am the light of the world"

Narrator

And so, once again this wonderful Christmas story is retold. It is a memorable and beautiful story. But what has Jesus, born 2022 years ago, got to do with our world and the way we live today?

Has he any more meaning in our lives, than just a legendary person? What would he mean to Adam and Eve if they were to come alive today and discover that he had been born?

(Adam and Eve stand up, looking rather puzzled and dazed.)

Adam and Eve, if they were alive today in the year 2022, would still find suffering, starvation, people wrongfully put in prison, people without homes and at war. They might at first think that Jesus had just come and then after being killed, had gone away again and so cannot make any difference to us. Quite clearly, he has not removed the hell on earth, so what has he done?

Adam and Eve might find out, and I say "might" because not many people do – that Jesus changes people, changes individuals, not in crowds and mass meetings, not in parades nor in vast assemblies, but Jesus knows each and every individual person, and He can change every person, because each single person matters to God. First, in all the other Apostles, Jesus brought light and hope. From that same light and hope the word of Jesus spread to others, and then to the faithful in every age, and so to the faithful in our world today.

(5 messengers of Hope come in, light candles and then kneel, holding up candles to represent the Church today.)

Narrator

Jesus comes to any person in pain. He comes through the care of anyone who visits him or her.
(One member who is from the pain group from the "Church" goes with candle and a pot of flowers to one of the congregation, puts flowers by them and sits with them.)

Narrator

Anyone in pain, or anyone who is suffering, feels the care given by another person. (And so the person in pain responds to the visitor). Very often he or she then looks to see how they can help others in pain. They realise that they too can show friendliness and compassion. (Now the person who was in pain turns to another person and washes face, combs hair of a person from the "Pain" Group.)

Narrator

In receiving and in giving care to others, hope grows in that person, and so anyone who is a disciple of Jesus today can pass on the hope that Jesus brought.

Someone representing the Pain Group lights a candle from Messenger's candle and goes to the Nativity scene, singing, to the tune of "O come let us adore Him", and says

"Christ gives me hope for ever".

(Another member of the 'Church' picks up a spade and bag of seeds and with his candle goes to the "Starvation" Group.)

Narrator

When we go among the starving, we take with us the hope and light of Christ. The light is given by the person who comes in Christ's name, who then tries to help him grow his own food and recover his self-respect.

(XYZ responds, shares the seeds with those around him, lights a candle from his helper and comes to the centre)

A member of Group 2

Christ gives me hope for ever

Narrator

In the loneliness of captivity, someone will now read to us of others, who, in Christ's name, have endured just such loneliness and misery for the sake of what is just and true. (One of those in prison, sits and reads.) But they endured it so bravely that they have made thousands respect them and the truth they stood for. Their lives bring hope to everyone. So, he prays (the reader kneels) and, in the hope Jesus brought, his soul takes wings, knowing that truth breaks down the barriers made of bars and chains; breaks down the barriers of race, creed and colour and gives everyone hope and light. Light more glorious than any daylight that we ever encounter, or the light that we are denied by being thrown into prison. (A third member of the "Church" goes to the prison, swings back a chair and lights a candle. A prisoner passes through the gap, singing ...)

Another member of Group 5 says

Christ gives me hope for ever.

Narrator

Among the faithful today, some look at the plight of the homeless and then, because they are followers of Jesus Christ, they provide housing and shelter. To anyone living with their family in one room, feeding, sleeping, washing in that one room, the offer of a home brings a new start, a new life.

(Another person from the "Church" takes a huge front door key and with a candle goes to the Refuge Group and gives the key to a couple in the Refuge Group.)

Narrator

As they realise that other people are working for their good, for them, hope comes again. It is the same hope that Jesus brought when he gave himself to all those around him.
(The couple light candles and move to the centre
Then as representatives of Group 4 they say together)

Christ gives us hope for ever.

Narrator

Against the backdrop of a mushroom cloud and staccato chatter of small arms fire, an army 'Private' reads a letter from home.

(A messenger from the "Church" brings a Letter and tears it open and reads a section from it.)

Narrator

To his despair, the soldier learns that a man called Ferdinand Ngusno with whom he has spent many happy hours, especially on the Athletics track, is a gunner in the army on the other side. He prays for his friend (he kneels) and finds an answer.

(Then he and Ferdinand Ngusno throw down their arms, move forward and shake hands. They light candles and go to the altar; pick up the cross; return to the crib and hold the cross over the crib.)

Narrator

And so, across the no man's land of war and human desolation, they meet and face each other; they ignore the puerile cries of politicians, because they know that the hope and light given by Christ matters more than the spin given by all those in politics. They understand that what they do might lead them from the Cradle to the Cross.

They sing together with the other group representatives

All Group members
Christ gives us hope forever
Christ gives us hope forever
Christ gives us hope forever
Christ the Lord

Officiant

Let us pray

O God, whose Son came into the world to combat hell on earth,
Give us hope to take the path of life that conquers hell by love.
Give us light to follow that path, however tortuous it becomes.
Give us courage to stick to that path, even though it takes us to a cross of our own.
We ask this through the man who was once the babe in Bethlehem, Jesus Christ Our Lord. Amen
(Officiant announces the final hymn)

To attune with the cry "Christ gives us hope for ever", we shall sing the hymn "O Come all ye Faithful".
(During the carol, which should if possible be sung by candlelight, the remainder of the groups light candles from their respective Messengers; go to the end of the nave and walk up in procession to the crib. They kneel.)

Reader 1
And God said, "Let there be light."

Reader 2
And Jesus said, "I am the light of the world."

The vicar The Blessing (lights go on) ...

And then (Invites everyone to come to the hall for refreshments)

The Giant Jigsaw

From God to Man

We have given this Service, which we affectionately refer to as the jigsaw service, the title From God to Man, and the Service is based on the script that follows.

The Bible

This Service presents the Old Testament with all its vitality; and shows that as a book the story is not completely told without the incarnation New Testament. It also goes on to show that the incarnation itself is incomplete without the resurrection. The Service is enormous fun, but needs much preparation. This, though, is a good use of time when there is so much teaching about the Bible involved.

The Script

The script needs to be studied carefully. Although it can be done without props, props are very helpful. Some are simple. For example, the wall of Jericho was built using large egg boxes piled high into a circle, with the children inside, so that when they are singing the relevant song, all other children shout "Hey" and those inside knock down the boxes and burst out; and don't they enjoy doing that!?

The Jigsaw

The jigsaw (shown on the next page) was an 8-foot by 4-foot piece of hardboard, with many pieces of polystyrene cut and fashioned / designed to the shape as shown, with the word GOD in blue. Small pins held the pieces in place.

Of the ten pieces that we used (more or less pieces are possible, of course), nine are for the Old Testament and only one is for the New Testament.

This one piece represents The Incarnation.

Each of the nine pieces is brought out, and put into position as the Old Testament sections unfolds.

Many children were involved, as shown below …

Jigsaw piece	1	God	Reader, Mr Jig The Saw
	2	Adam and Eve	Adam, Eve and Serpent
	3	Noah	The very young children, dressed up as animals
	4	Abraham	presented through a Poem
	5	Jacob and Joseph	Jacob, Joseph, Ten Brothers

6	Moses	Pharaoh, Moses, Slaves
7	Judges	Joshua and Soldiers
8	Kings	David
9	Prophets	A Reader
10	The Incarnation	Readers, Mary and Joseph Three Kings, Shepherds, and Angels

The jigsaw is turned over to show The Picture on the reverse side.

The Picture

On the reverse side of the jigsaw, one of the congregation had painted a manger in the centre; this was superimposed on a simple cross, which extended to all edges, leaving four spaces, in which were painted people living and working in our own community, in whom Christ can be seen today. Mirrors also were glued onto the picture so that people could see themselves and ask of themselves, "Is Christ risen in me?"

The Resurrection

For the presentation of the resurrection, the local junior school produced two short dramas to demonstrate the way in which they saw the risen Christ in people that they had identified, sometimes from the present day, other times from the pages of history.

This Jigsaw method can, of course, be used for many other Christian themes. For example, it could be used to produce another drama about (say) Martin Luther King.

On, or perhaps in front of the altar there needs to be erected the frame to hold the jigsaw, in our case 8 feet by 4 feet. The pieces will be kept at the back of the Church, guarded by Mr Jig the Saw:

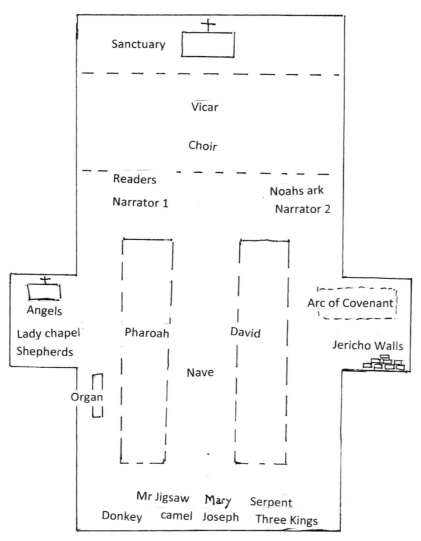

This diagram shows everyone's position at the beginning of the Service

The ten pieces of the Jigsaw had already been cut out and then they are assembled in the way shown in the diagram below; but, of course, you can use any design that you wish:

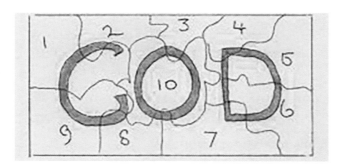

On the other side of the Jigsaw was depicted the six following images:

The Incarnation	A manger
The Crucifixion	A cross
The Resurrection	Mirrors (to represent today)

You will also need as many of the following as possible ...
staging in the Chancel and at the Chancel steps
a two-dimensional Noah's Ark by the pulpit
a three-dimensional Ark of the Covenant
a live (or pretend) donkey
a full-size pretend camel
a pretend serpent

3. The Jigsaw will be built up as each of the sections / titles below are completed.

"FROM GOD TO MAN"

Before the Service starts

There will be an introduction to the music used in the Service. This will be played on the organ and also on some musical instruments, played by the children.

THE SERVICE

Narrator ... Let me introduce this service to you.

The Bible is a complicated, long, and sometimes frightening book. It is so long and so complicated that few of us ever really read and understand it. It has a history that is glorious and yet bedevilled with bloodshed. It has inspired millions. One such person was Martin Luther, who used its teaching to correct some of the wrongdoings and thinking in the Church of God of his day. The Bible has also provoked tragedy. William Tyndale, about 450 years ago, translated the Bible into English and was burnt at the stake for doing so. Even today, if you smuggle Bibles into communist countries, you may end up in prison.

Many of us feel guilty about our lack of knowledge of the Bible because we do not grasp what it is about. We feel guilty, because we become muddled with the detail – like the child who once wrote that King Solomon had many wives and a thousand porcupines!

So, today, we hope that as we present this Service, we are able to see the wood for the trees; to see the pattern of the Bible; to understand how gradually God revealed himself to man over many centuries, and how it took a long time for man to properly understand the nature of God… a process that still continues today.

And, because we are all so puzzled, we shall use the jigsaw puzzle to help us. After each piece of the Old Testament is put into place, we shall then fit in another piece of the puzzle, and then another. Then we will show that, at the end of the Old. Testament, we need something more to complete the puzzle. Hence … our title and our theme.

"FROM GOD TO MAN"

Jig-Saw Piece No 1   GOD

Narrator
So, let's start with the opening words of the Bible.
We shall ask a very young reader to climb the steps to the lectern and read the first four words:

Young Reader
"In the beginning God"

Narrator
And in goes the first piece of the puzzle

Jig-Saw Piece No 2   ADAM AND EVE

Narrator
Once upon a time, as all good stories start, there was a man called Adam.
    (Adam rises slowly from the floor of the Chancel)
    He was a man who lived happily in his beautiful surroundings. He lived at peace and the whole of his life was good; for he lived close to God in the Garden of Eden.
    Chorus "Man at peace with God in Eden"
    (This continues quietly and steadily as background rhythm, until the fruit-picking scene)

Narrator

He was given a companion, Eve, with whom to share his life. (Eve walks out and joins Adam) And, in sharing his life with someone else, he became even more happy and joyful. (Adam and Eve hold hands)

And so, this story might have ended, as some good stories do, with Adam and Eve living happily ever after.

But this was not to be. For in their happy existence, Adam and Eve had to obey one rule – and that was not to eat of the fruit of the tree of knowledge.

But in the story we are told that a serpent tempted Eve to break that rule and evil came into their lives, in the form of a serpent.

(Serpent starts to slide forward to the counter-chorus)

Counter-Chorus

Evil ... Evil ... Evil. (Continuously harmonising with the previous chorus rendition)
"Man at peace with God in Eden".

(As Eve and the serpent touch, there is sudden silence and, in this silence, Eve reaches up to the fruit, withdraws her hand, hesitates and reaches up again. She plucks the fruit, holds it in her hands and then suddenly takes a bite. She smiles and hands it to Adam, who looks both horrified and fascinated. He slowly raises the fruit and then he takes a bite.

(Immediate LOUD NOISE – drums, organ, percussion by the Musicians)

Narrator

At this moment man fell, man succumbed to temptation! He knew good but chose evil, and so was cast out of the Garden of Eden into the world.

(In goes jigsaw piece No 2)

Jigsaw Piece No 3   NOAH

Narrator

And in those long ago and almost forgotten days, men and women behaved very badly. Men and women "fell" with such a tremendous thunder-like crash (metaphorically speaking), that God felt angry with them, and sick of the sight of man and woman, so He singled out the one good man left in the world – Noah – and told him what he should do ... he should build an ...

(Ask young children for the answer ... **Ark**)

This story of the Ark we do, of course, all know. We know it well enough to realise that the song we are about to sing is inaccurate; but it is fun, and it's sung to enable some of the younger people present to act out the story.

So, we'll sing "And they all went into the Ark".

1. The animals went in one by one, hurrah, hurrah

    The animals went in one by one, hurrah, hurrah

    The animals went in one by one,

    The elephant chewing a caraway bun,

    And they all went into the ark,

    For to get out of the rain

2. The animals went in two by two

    The Rhinoceros and the Kangaroo

3. The animals went in three by three

    The bear, the bug and the bumblebee

4. The animals went in four by four

    The great hippopotamus stuck in the door

5. The animals went in five by five

    With Wellington boots they did arrive

6. The animals went in six by six

    The hyena laughed at the monkeys' tricks

7. The animals went in seven by seven

    Said the ant to the elephant, "Who are you shoving?"

8. The animals went in eight by eight

    They came with a rush, 'cos it was so late

9. The animals went in nine by nine

    Old Noah shouted, "Cut that line"

10. The animals went in ten by ten

    The Ark, she blew her whistle then

11. And then the voyage it did begin

    Old Noah pulled the gangplank in

12. They never knew where they were at

    Till the old ark bumped on Ararat.

(During this song, if possible some of those younger members can be dressed as animals and they can process up the steps and into the ark at the pulpit steps. If you wish them to, they can then disappear out of sight, go out of, say, the East Door, and make their way back to the Congregation via the main or West Door)

(In the last verse, in goes Jigsaw piece No 3)

Jigsaw Piece No 4   ABRAHAM

Narrator
God promised Abraham that he would give Palestine to Abraham and his descendants. Thus, it became (and in the eyes of the Jews, still is) "The Promised Land".
We are now going to hear a bit of verse on the subject.

Reader
Abraham saw two Angels come.
They said "One day you'll have a son;
And from your family,
God will raise an almighty nation
to give Him praise."

(In goes Piece No 4)

Jigsaw Piece No 5   JACOB AND JOSEPH

Reader
Abraham, then Isaac, then Jacob his lad.
Jacob and Rachel with twelve sons were glad
But his brothers nine to Egypt, Joseph sold
Where he, of a famine, Pharaoh told.

Narrator
Yes, Abraham's son, Isaac, had Jacob. Then Jacob had many sons, but one favourite, Joseph, to whom he gave a coat of many colours, with disastrous consequences. Let sing about it now:

Joseph's brothers were not too pleased with what they saw
They had never liked him much before
And now this coat had got their goat
They felt life was unfair
And when Joseph graced the scene
His brothers turned a shade of green
His astounding clothing took the biscuit
Quite the smoothest person in the district
He looked handsome; he looked smart
He was a walking work of art.

Such a dazzling coat of many colours
How he loved his coat of many colours
It was red and yellow and green and brown and scarlet
And black and purple and pink and orange and blue.

(During this, Joseph comes up to Jacob, on stage. The old man mimes the giving of the coat. Joseph then dances and cartwheels down and up the aisle twice. Joseph finishes on the stage, surrounded by the angry brothers, who are holding long coloured sticks, and they hold these sticks to form 'prison bars')
And so, the brothers, in their jealousy, sold Joseph into Egypt. And Joseph found himself in prison.

Joseph in Prison

All Sing
Close every door to me, hide all the world from me
Bar all my windows and shut out the light.
Do what you want with me, hate me and laugh at me
Darken my daytime and torture my night.
If my life were important, I would ask will I live or die
But I know the answers lie far from this world.
Close every door to me, keep those I love from me
Children of Israel are never alone.
For I know I shall find my own peace of mind
For I have been promised a land of my own.

Narrator
But Joseph got out of prison, made a good life for himself in Egypt, and, under Pharaoh, the King of Egypt, Joseph controlled all the food in Egypt. Famine in their own country drove his brothers to Egypt, where, eventually, they were welcomed.

(In goes Piece No 5)

Jigsaw Piece No 6   MOSES

Narrator
A few generations later, the Jews in Egypt had been made slaves and needed Moses, who, under God's guidance, freed them and led them back to the 'Promised Land'. Moses saw the persecution of his brothers and sisters.

(Spontaneous Drama using as many slaves as you can muster. Slaves come down the aisle; two groups on their knees, heaving an imaginary or polystyrene block of stone, while slave-drivers walk up and down between them. These slave-drivers shout "HEAVE" – and then WHIP the slaves ... repeat ... repeat)

Moses confronts Pharaoh and says
    "Let my people go"

Adult Chorus sings ...

1.	Let my people go	(Children start to clap at line 5)
2.	Let my people go	
3.	Let my people go	
4.	Let my people go	
5.	Let my people go	Clap, clap, clap,
6.	Let my people go	Clap, clap, clap,

All clap and chant

1.   Let's go (loud)
2.   Let's go (louder)
3.   Let's go (loudest)
4.   Let's go (shout)
5.   Let's go (yell)
6.   Let' s go (raise the roof!)

(In goes Jigsaw piece No 6)

Jigsaw Piece No 7   JUDGES

Narrator
And so they did. They went. They left Egypt and went through the Red Sea and into the Wilderness for a generation. Moses died, but Joshua led them into the Promised Land.

    And all the way there, they were carrying the Ark of the Covenant, with the tablets of Law – The Ten Commandments – inside. Moreover, they also flattened the walls of Jericho.

    <u>(While some people act out Joshua and the fighting of the Battle of Jericho, everyone else sings)</u>

Chorus
Joshua fight de battle of Jericho, Jericho, Jericho,
Joshua fight de battle of Jericho,
An' de walls come tumbling down

Verse 1
You may talk about yo' king of Gideon,
You may talk about yo' man of Saul,
There's none like good ol' Joshua
An' de battle of Jericho

Chorus
Joshua fight de battle of Jericho, Jericho, Jericho,
Joshua fight de battle of Jericho,
An' de walls come tumbling down

Verse 2
Up to de walls of Jericho
He marched with spear in hand,
"Go blow dem rams' horns', Joshua cried,
"Cos de battle am in my hands"

Chorus
Joshua fight de battle of Jericho, Jericho, Jericho,
Joshua fight de battle of Jericho,
An' de walls come tumbling down

Verse 3
Den the lam-ram sheep horns 'gin to blow,
Trumpets begin to sound,
Joshua commanded de children to shout "HEY" very loud
An' de walls come tumbling down

Chorus
Joshua fight de battle of Jericho, Jericho, Jericho,
Joshua fight de battle of Jericho,
An' de walls come tumbling down

(And in goes Jigsaw piece No 7)

Jigsaw piece No 8   KINGS

Narrator

Throughout history there were many people who were appointed as judges who were the leaders of Israel, and they were followed by many anointed Kings. Samuel, the last of the judges, anointed Saul the first of the Kings. Saul was followed by King David, who, as a shepherd boy, killed Goliath. King David wrote psalms and he also captured Jerusalem. When he brought the ark there, he was so thrilled that he danced in front of it.

So, we shall sing a psalm (No 150) to a modern setting, while David dances before the ark.

PSALM 150

1. O praise God in his holiness: praise him in the firmament of his power.
2. Praise him in his noble acts: praise him according to his excellent greatness.
3. Praise him in the sound of the trumpet: praise him upon the lute and harp.
4. Praise him in the cymbals and dances: praise him upon the strings and pipe.
5. Praise him upon the well-tuned cymbals: praise him upon the loud cymbals.
6. Let everything that hath breath praise the Lord.

(And in goes Jigsaw piece No 8)

Jigsaw Piece No 9   The PROPHETS

Narrator

King David was followed as King by his son Solomon, who, apart from his porcupines (his concubines!!), built the Temple in Jerusalem. Later, some of the Kings quarrelled and this led to infighting, and the Jewish empire being split up ... just as has happened in Ireland and many other countries.

Prophets came to upbraid the kings and also the people for their selfishness. Prophets such as Elijah, Elisha, Jeremiah, Amos, Micah and others, but, in particular, we remember a prophet who looked to the future: he was called Isaiah.

Reader

(Chap 9:6) And Isaiah told the people …

        For to us a child is born, to us a son is given;

        and the government will be upon his shoulder,

and his name will be called
"Wonderful Counsellor, Mighty God,
Everlasting Father, Prince of Peace."

(And in goes Jigsaw piece No 9)

Jigsaw piece No 10   THE INCARNATION

Narrator
And so to demonstrate the fulfilment of that prophecy that we have just heard, we will start with the Carol "Unto us a boy is born!"

All sing　　　Unto us a boy is born!

READING　　Luke 1 (26-31)　　　THE ANNUNCIATION

Carol　　　"O little town of Bethlehem"　verses 1, 2, 3 and 5

(During this, Mary rides on the donkey up the aisle. Joseph is with her)

Reading　　Luke 2 (1-7)　　　THE BIRTH

(During this, the final piece of Jigsaw is fitted, No 10)

THE SHEPHERDS

Carol "While Shepherds watched."
(During this, Angels and Shepherds come forward to the "Stable")

THE KINGS

The World comes to Jesus

READING　　Matthew 2 (1-29 10-12)

CAROL　　　"We Three Kings"

(During this, the 3 Kings come forward on the camel)

Would it be difficult to disguise him as a camel?

Reader

So Jesus comes into the World.

And we see and hear two SHORT DRAMAS, illustrating how Jesus can be born in human beings today.

We look at: 1. "THE PLAGUE AT EYAM"
                      2. "GLADYS AYLWARD IN CHINA"

(It is very easy to read about these two historic times, and create your own drama to use at this point in the Service. And, of course, you may decide to choose others)

The Turning-Round of the Jigsaw

Priest explains

We have the picture of:

1. The Incarnation showing God giving to us everything that we have, and this includes
2. First, the gift of Jesus
3. The Crucifixion   Christ giving His life for us
4. The Resurrection   We are given New Life
5. And finally we give this New Life ... Our new life ... back to God

*This is not a picture. These are mirrors, in which we see ourselves. If we will let him do so, Jesus lives in us. This is the Resurrection today.

PRAYERS ... Led by members of the Congregation

PROCESSIONAL   Hymn: "O Come all ye faithful"
(Everyone in Church will be invited to process up to the altar, look in the mirror and ask themselves the question "Do I see Christ living in me, this Christmas?")

The Vicar   THE BLESSING

AND THEN THE ENTIRE CAST TAKE A BOW
... ALL IS FINISHED

111

SECTION 3
MISCELLANEOUS IDEAS

MUSIC

Children will respond positively to an invitation to produce their own music, or at the very least to suggest the kind of music they feel they wish to be included in worship. They will come up with all kinds of ideas and suggestions.

For example, did you know that you can sing …

"While shepherds watched their flocks by night" to the tune of "Match of the Day"! Indeed, for them to play the tune for it to be sung to, they just need to learn three chords! Borrow as many guitars as possible, and teach the children E, B flat, and A. Moreover, as the children play and sing the carol there are only seven chord changes in eight lines of verse.

These are …
While (E) shepherds watched their flocks by night
All seated on the (Bf) ground,
The Angel of the Lord came down, and glory shone around.
"Fear not," said he (for mighty dread
Had seized their troubled (A) mind);
"Glad tidings of great (E) joy I bring
To (Bf) you and all mankind."

If they are happier in the key of D, then the tune can be transposed to the chords of D – Af – G.

Then, of course, it is possible to include in this, and any other songs, any other instruments you can lay your hands on … recorders, chime – bars, triangles, glockenspiel, drums etc. It is very easy to make maracas out of containers and rice. If there are children who are reluctant to become involved, they can be given the simplest of instruments to play, or they can be asked to introduce a carol.

Most children are really thrilled to be 'in the orchestra', even if they do no more than hit a drum once in a verse. Viz: In the carol "Celebrations", a drumbeat is a great addition at one particular point, just at the rest, before the words of the last line "There's a new King …"

CAROLS

All traditional carols are popular. Many of them can be acted or mimed. Children and their parents will nearly always respond to an invitation to be creative, and in both Churches and schools we have, for example, seen a myriad of superb camels, and of all shapes and sizes, carrying the "Kings" on their backs! It remains one of our unfulfilled ambitions to have a real camel in Church. Maybe you have a zoo nearby?

Some modern carols are attached at Appendix B. They have instant appeal to young people.

MOVEMENT TO DRUMBEAT

The word "dance" is anathema to many boys, but we have found that teenage boys may well take a very different view if they are asked to make their dance movements to drumbeat. One staccato bang on a drum, and the boys will move instantly and freeze until the next drum beat. Vivid drama can be portrayed in this way, either with a commentary, or with no other sound except that coming from the drum.

THE PARTY AFTER THE SERVICE

It was Edward Patey who, when he was Dean of Liverpool, said, "The Church should be a laboratory for relationships."

We know from our own experience that it is the cup of coffee or tea after Parish Eucharist which becomes an integral part of the morning worship, and during this time great ideas will emerge, and deep and lasting friendships can be formed. We believe that after any one of the Services in this book, and as set out above, some kind of party afterwards is an appropriate way to celebrate all that has taken place.

Parents will always respond generously if they are asked to produce sausage rolls, crisps, and mince pies. Members of the Church will be prepared to organise soft drinks and tea and coffee for all those who choose to stay.

So that the adults can continue to interact after the party – even perhaps over the washing up! – it is worthwhile having something to distract the children … something that does not need too much organising, not least because the Service itself will have been pretty extending.

Some possible ideas to do this are:

1 **A Video or YouTube film,** which are very easy to organise, or a homemade film of the Sunday School or Church outing, perhaps shot in the previous summer.

   All children love to see themselves on the screen.

2 **A Film or something a little different.** There are many superb cartoon films, including one called "When the Littlest Camel Knelt". It has an amusing tape / cassette to go with it.

   You will, of course, have your own computer system with in-built projector, but if not, one can almost certainly be borrowed from one of the local schools, as can a screen. Most Churches have areas within them that are dark enough for projection.

The Film (or any other) mentioned above can be downloaded, or even still be bought … Simply Google it.

MUSIC AGAIN

As mentioned earlier, we use a great number of carols and other music to bring children to life. There are many books of modern carols which children love, and will quickly learn if they haven't come across them before.

A Christmas Action Song A really 'fun' way to finish the party is with "The Twelve Days of Christmas", sung and acted by everyone, including all the adults. Suggested actions which have stood the test of time are given later in this chapter.

Some further suggestions as to songs / music for Christmas that you will find can be quickly learned and will be loved …

1. It's The Most Wonderful Time Of The Year
2. Calypso Carol
3. Carol Of The Drum
4. Carol Of The Bells
5. Chestnuts Roasting On An Open Fire
6. Driving Home For Christmas
7. White Christmas
8. It's Beginning To Look A Lot Like Christmas
9. Santa Baby
10. O Holy Night
11. Mary's Boy Child
12. Wonderful Christmastide
13. Have Yourself A Merry Little Christmas
14. Santa Claus Is Coming To Town
15. Celebrations … by Valerie Collinson
16. Sing A Song … by Kenneth Forrest
17. Carol Gaily Carol … by Valerie Collinson
18. Gentle Shepherd … By Lynne Tregarthen and Richard Riley

To find the music and the words for all the above, simply Google them.

Events that you can organise / 'put on' to keep the troops entertained

1. Design and make an order card (see illustration)
2. Write an Invitation Letter (see illustration)
3. Devise a registration card (see illustration)
4. Meet Father Christmas
5. Organise a Nativity Play
6. Sardines
7. Dressed up 'hide and seek'

Games that can be played

1. **Make your own crib**

   The first game that I would suggest would be to 'Make your own crib'. Divide all those taking part into teams. For example, if there are fifteen children, then three sets of five children would work well. You then need three sets of crib figures, each piece labelled team A, team B, etc ... one set for each team.

   Begin by someone hiding the crib figures. You might need one person per team to do this. Once this has been done for all the teams, then give the 'All clear', and allow the teams to search for them and find them. The task is for every team to find every one of their figures (perhaps 15 in total) and then build their own crib. Judging can be done on a number of different bases. E.g., the first team to finish. Or the most attractive crib. Etc.

2. **The story writing game**

   Give each team a set of 20 words, each set on printed cards; for example, 'Heavens, Cattle, Angel, baby, door, etc' ... Then ask them to write their own story that must incorporate all the words, and also relate to Christmas.

3. **The sweetie hunt**

   If you are expecting, say, 30 children, and intending to divide them into 5 teams of 6 children, then head to the sweet shop and buy 100 sweets. This should be five sets of sweets, with each set in a different colour. Before the game starts, hide the 100 sweets, and then divide the children into teams of six. Then, on the word 'GO', each team finds their own set of twenty sweets, and the winner is the team who do so in the shortest time.

4. **The dressing-up game**
    For this you are going to need a huge bag of dressing-up clothes, and a whole range of other props. (See below.)

    Divide all those who are intending to be players into teams of three. Give each team a bag of clothes and other props, such as a sword, a bell, a pint jug or tankard.

    Each team should then choose one of their number and dress them up as … an angel,

    or a soldier, or the innkeeper, or perhaps Mary,

    or it could be Joseph, or even a camel, etc.

    When all the teams are finished, then ask all the players to guess who each team has chosen to try to replicate.

5. **The Letters game**
    Once again divide your group of players into teams of three. Give each team a bag of one hundred letters. These are easily printed, but you need to make sure that you have the right number of consonants, etc, and only a small number of the difficult vowels. (So, for example, five E's, four A's, but only one J, etc.)

    Each team is then set the task of making as many words as they can that relate to the Christmas story, e.g. Crib, stable, baby, camel, king, shepherd, etc.

    Once they have used a letter in a particular word, it cannot be used again. The best way of achieving this is for all the words to stay intact until the end of the game.

    When you call 'time', the winner is the team which has made the most words, or perhaps used the most letters.

6. **The Christmas 'Mimes' game**
    Every person who is 'on' must choose a character from the Biblical Christmas story, and then use

the usual 'Miming method' to describe that character. So, of course, no speaking. Just the usual actions until someone guesses who is being portrayed.

7. Chocolate coin game

You will need a plentiful supply of chocolate coins covered in the usual gold foil and which are readily available from most confectionery shops. At the same time, buy a Chocolate Selection Box, and place either on a table or on the floor. Get the children and other participants to roll gold-coloured coins towards a selection box and, of course, the nearest to the box wins the box of chocolates.

8. Chocolate bar frenzy

Without question this is one of the most popular games of all. You will need to assemble: hats, gloves, scarf, a knife and fork, and a dice (if you have access to a very large die, so much the better), together with a large chocolate bar, which must be left in its wrapper, and can even have further paper wrappings added!!

Each player in turn rolls the dice. When you roll a six, you are 'it'.

You grab the hat, scarf and gloves, and put them on as quickly as possible, then take the knife and fork, and attack the chocolate bar, trying to get through the paper coverings and eat as much as you can. In the meantime, all the other players continue to roll the dice, and as soon as the next player rolls a six, he or she 'undresses' you, and then immediately dons the hat, scarf and gloves and attacks the chocolate.

And so it continues until the entire bar has been consumed ... or time runs out!

9. Christmas-themed banana gram

Bananagrams is a wonderful high-speed game, but when used at a Christmas party only words to do with the nativity story are allowed. Everyone knows how to play the normal game, of course, but now each person is trying to find only words that can be justified as a word from the Christmas story ... Bethlehem, Nazareth, Star, Crib, Angel, Mary, Joseph, Ox, Ass, Camel, Straw, Manger, Stable, etc.

When the winner calls "BANANAS", the game ends and the winner must justify each word that they have assembled. If any word is not accepted, then this person's tiles are put back into the mix and the game continues.

It can take forever!!

10. Secret Santa

You will need to do some preparation, but this can be great fun at a Church Christmas party, especially if the party follows a Service at which everyone has been taking part.

You will need the following:

Pens and paper. Some pre-bought gifts, such as oranges, apples, bars of chocolate, packets of sweets, wrapping paper, Sellotape, gift tags, cards with envelopes, etc.

Round 1 … Ask each person playing the game to write their name on a piece of paper, and then put all the names into a bag or hat, and allow each participant to draw one name out … secretly. (If anyone should draw out their own name, then put the piece of paper back into the bag and draw another.)

Round 2 … Once everyone has another person's name, then they should choose a gift from the pile that you have assembled, choosing something that they believe is most appropriate for the person destined to receive it. They should then wrap it up and put a gift tag on it, and label it with the name of the person for whom it is intended. Then also write a card for the same person, put it into the envelope and address it.

Round 3 … The organiser now gives out all the gifts and the cards.

Round 4 … Each of the players is allowed three questions to any of the players and tries to identify the giver of the gift.

11. Puppet Shows

How well I remember sitting on the sands with mum and dad during our Summer seaside holiday, watching a puppet show … usually a one-man affair with a canvas booth and the puppeteer inside with six or seven puppets or marionettes.

Children can have enormous fun making their own puppets or marionettes, and then putting on a puppet show, and if it is a marionette show then a special stage needs to be created.

It is very easy to recreate any one of a number of scenes from the Christmas birth narrative as a puppet show.

For example: The archangel's visit to Mary, in which case the puppets that would need making are the Archangel, Mary and Joseph.

And if the scene to be depicted was 'No room at the inn', then the puppets to make for this would be the Innkeeper, Mary and Joseph, and perhaps one or two animals.

For the birth of Jesus, the puppets to make would be Mary, Joseph, Jesus (as a baby), an Ox, and an Ass.

For a scene depicting the visit of the shepherds to the manger, you would need to make Mary, Joseph, the baby Jesus, perhaps two shepherds and a lamb.

If you are trying to recreate the Magi arriving from the East and then giving their gifts to Jesus, then the puppets to make would be Mary, Joseph, baby Jesus, 3 Magi, with each of them holding their gift of gold, frankincense, myrrh, and which need to be able to be detached from the Magi and put down in front of Jesus ... and if you can manage to lay your hands on a camel!!

The journey of the Magi might be a little more difficult.

But one could make a brave attempt with such puppets as the three Magi, a travelling Star, three Camels, King Herod, and one or two of Herod's advisers and also a stable door.

Pictures that can be created / coloured
This is probably the easiest game / diversion of all to arrange, but is especially useful when you are trying to distract a large group of young children. You need crayons, or coloured pens or pencils (paint is very messy in a large group) and either A3 or A4 sheets of paper, or pre-printed 'Nativity scenes'. Give each child ten or fifteen minutes to create their own picture.

We have found it works extremely well to have the pictures sequential, starting with the annunciation to Mary, then the journey to Bethlehem, the entrance to the stable, the birth of Jesus, and so on.

When all the pictures are completed, they can be blu-tacked onto a wall to make a frieze, and so tell the entire story of the birth, just as many historical tapestries do.

People dress up as ...
What fun ... You will need simply a large bag of clothes, shoes, hats, implements such as swords and wings, and a bag in which are pieces of paper with pre-printed names on them. Let each child draw out a name, and then give them ten minutes to find the appropriate clothes etc, and dress up accordingly, such as:

1. Centurion (as the taxes are paid)
2. Innkeeper (with door knocker?)
3. King Herod
4 Mary
5. Joseph
6. Shepherds

When the dressing up has finished, you can then either have a procession, or a tableau, or even re-enact the birth of Jesus story!!

13 . JIGSAWS

It can be a simple matter to create a giant jigsaw.

This can be made either from a large sheet of thin plywood, or MDF, obtainable at any DIY store, and can be as large as 8 foot x 4 foot (2.4m x 1.2m).

One of the Church members could then paint it with a nativity scene.

Another member could cut it into, say, between 10 and 32 jigsaw pieces and hide each piece in or around the outside of the Church or school or Church hall.

Then, during the sermon slot, or youth club or school talk, children will head off, find all the pieces, and re-assemble the immense jigsaw, talking about the picture / theme as they do so. You can also consider hiding the central piece in a remote hideaway, and only when the jigsaw has been completely assembled except for this one piece, give away clues as to the location of the last piece.

When it is brought in, and added as the final piece, this gives a perfect opportunity to use this moment to create the 'climax' to the whole event.

NB. A large blackboard or painting stand … a large blackboard easel, or painting stand might be very useful

14 Appendix

The words and actions for The Twelve Days of Christmas

On the first day of Christmas my true love sent to me
A partridge in a pear tree

On the second day of Christmas my true love sent to me
Two turtle doves
And a partridge in a pear tree

On the third day of Christmas my true love sent to me
Three French hens
Two turtle doves and a partridge in a pear tree

On the fourth day of Christmas my true love sent to me
Four calling birds, Three French hens
Two turtle doves and a partridge in a pear tree

On the fifth day of Christmas my true love sent to me
Five gold rings, Four calling birds, Three French hens
Two turtle doves and a partridge in a pear tree

On the sixth day of Christmas my true love sent to me
Six geese a-laying, Five gold rings, Four calling birds
Three French hens, Two turtle doves and a partridge in a pear tree

On the seventh day of Christmas my true love sent to me
Seven swans a-swimming, Six geese a-laying, Five gold rings,
Four calling birds, Three French hens,
Two turtle doves and a partridge in a pear tree

On the eighth day of Christmas my true love sent to me
Eight maids a-milking, Seven swans a-swimming, Six geese a-laying,
Five gold rings, Four calling birds, Three French hens,
Two turtle doves and a partridge in a pear tree

On the ninth day of Christmas my true love sent to me
Nine drummers drumming, Eight maids a-milking,

Seven swans a-swimming, Six geese a-laying, Five gold rings
Four calling birds, Three French hens
Two turtle doves and a partridge in a pear tree

On the tenth day of Christmas my true love sent to me
Ten pipers piping, Nine drummers drumming, Eight maids a-milking,
Seven swans a-swimming, Six geese a-laying, Five gold rings,
Four calling birds, Three French hens
Two turtle doves and a partridge in a pear tree

On the eleventh day of Christmas my true love sent to me
Eleven ladies dancing, Ten pipers piping, Nine drummers drumming,
Eight maids a-milking, Seven swans a-swimming, Six geese a-laying
Five gold rings, Four calling birds, Three French hens
Two turtle doves and a partridge in a pear tree

On the twelfth day of Christmas my true love sent to me
Twelve Lords a-leaping, Eleven ladies dancing, Ten pipers piping
Nine drummers drumming, Eight maids a-milking,
Seven swans a-swimming, Six geese a-laying
Five gold rings, Four calling birds, Three French hens
Two turtle doves and a partridge in a pear tree

THE ACTIONS
On the first day of Christmas (Action – Point up at the tree)

On the second day of Christmas (Action – Hold up two index fingers and then link them)

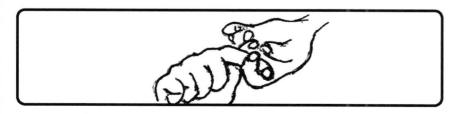

On the third day of Christmas (Action – Hold up three fingers)

On the fourth day of Christmas (Action – Cup hands round mouth and shout "4 calling birds")

On the fifth day of Christmas (Action – With the arms, make 5 Olympic circles in the air)

On the sixth day of Christmas (Action – With index finger and thumb of each hand, make the shape of a very large egg)

On the seventh day of Christmas (Action – Paddle like mad with arms flailing up and down)

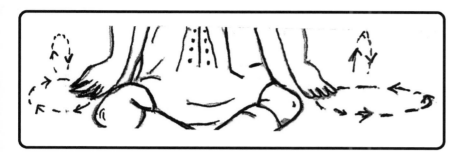

On the eighth day of Christmas (Action – No milking machines here. So pump up and down with your hands for that pinta!)

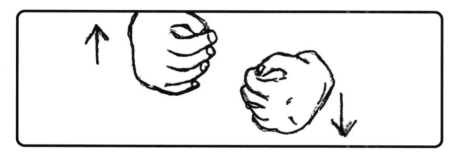

On the ninth day of Christmas (Action – Beat up and down on an imaginary drum)

On the tenth day of Christmas (Action – Both hands up to mouth; move fingers as if playing pipes)

On the eleventh day of Christmas (Action – Ladies & Girls only. Stand up, hand on head, and twirl)

On the twelfth day of Christmas (Action – Men and Boys, your turn. Jump up and reach for the ceiling)

An invitation (to as many homes in the area as you can manage)

In this modern world of iPhones and emails, people love
receiving letters delivered by the Postman. So one possible way
to try to persuade people to come to the Church,
or the village hall, might be by way of a personal invitation.
We managed to deliver six thousand letters to every home
in the parish in the two weeks before Christmas
(we asked 60 people to deliver 100 letters each).
And the response was great. The front of the letter read:

BY ORDER OF

His Most Imperial Majesty
CAESAR AUGUSTUS
You are to pay your taxes on
23rd December at 3.30pm
*In Bethlehem ***

Book your room at the Inn now!!

*** If you cannot make it to Bethlehem.*
St John's Church will do.

The reverse of the letter explained our temerity.

So, as the recipient opened the envelope and unfolded the letter, it had been inserted so that they read the reverse side first (see below).

This is not a letter from the Inland Revenue (!!) but from St John's to all those living in the parish.

You are probably familiar with St Luke's Gospel story of Joseph and Mary coming to Bethlehem to be taxed, and whilst they were there Mary giving birth to Jesus Christ in a stable.

At St John's we shall be recalling the story vividly and we are inviting you to be part of it.

When you arrive, register at the door with the Roman soldiers and pay your taxes!

(In this case, what you would like to give for God's work this Christmas.)

The time is 3.30pm on Sunday 23rd December at St John's. After the Service, at about 4.15pm, we shall go in torchlight procession to sing carols with the elderly residents of Pool Grange.

You would be welcome also at:
    11.30pm Christmas Eve   – The Midnight Mass
    9.30am Christmas Day   – Family Service with Communion

With best wishes from all of us at St John's.

And at the 3.30pm Christmas Eve Service, those who responded were greeted at the door by ...

A phalanx of Roman soldiers, 21 of them, dressed as in the picture below, in gold and silver card (obtained from a local cigarette factory). The centurion, a 6ft 3in boy in his teens, stood with helmet on at 7 feet high ... magnificent.

The solders gave each person coming in a pen, an envelope and a registration card.

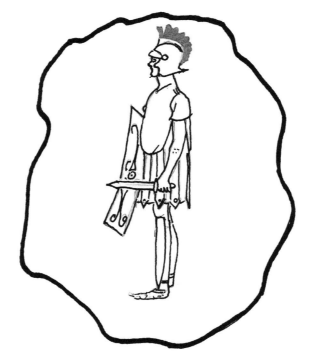

"How many of these costumes do you say that I need to make?"

REGISTRATION CARD

Please complete this card and hand it in,
with your envelope, to the centurion or his soldiers
during the registration hymn....The First Nowell.

****

This is to say that, in response to the summons to be taxed,
I/We have given an offering to God, this Christmas 1979.

Name of Individual/Family

....

Address

....

The Service ran as follows:

1. Introit Hymn: "Once in Royal David's City"
2. Introduction to the service by the Vicar
3. Hymn: "Hark the Herald Angels Sing"
    (The soldiers marched to their posts during the singing of this hymn ... which were seven tables positioned strategically around the Church. (A phalanx of soldiers marching up the aisle remains an unforgettable sight.)
4. First Reading: Luke 2 (1 to 3) "The Emperor's Decree"
5. Registration Hymn: "The First Nowell"
    During this hymn, everyone was 'marshalled / escorted by the soldiers to all the tables and asked to hand in their card and envelope
6. The Service then followed the usual Nativity pattern, but could, of course, also be followed by a 'Blessing of the crib' service or 'A Christingle' or a 'Carol Service'